The Little Book of

GRAND PRIX LEGENDS

PHILIP RABY

The Little Book of

GRAND PRIX LEGENDS

This edition first published in the UK in 2006
By Green Umbrella

www.greenumbrella.co.uk

Publishers Jules Gammond, Tim Exell, Vanessa Gardner

Printed and bound in China

ISBN 1-905009-82-8

zepter
cosmetics
Marlboro
Marlboro
Marlboro
Marlboro
Marlboro
MONACO
Grand Prix
PETROBRAS
Panasonic

CONTENTS

CONTENTS

FERNANDO ALONSO

Nationality: Spanish
Born: 1981
Seasons: 2001-
Teams: Minardi, Renault
World Titles: 1 (2005)

Did you know?

As Spain's first successful Formula One driver, Fernando Alonso is massively popular in that country, a phenomenon that's been dubbed 'Alonsomania'. He has created a resurgence of interest in the sport in his home country.

The newest name in Formula One is also one of the sport's most exciting newcomers and he is already pegged to be the next Michael Schumacher. And for good reason, too, because in 2005 Fernando Alonso won the World Drivers' Championship, breaking Schumacher's reign and becoming the youngest ever driver to win the title, at just 24 years of age.

Impressive stuff, and all thanks to his father's passion for kart racing. Like many parents, Spanish explosives expert, José Luis, wanted his children to take on his hobby. So he built his eight-year-old daughter a simple kart but she took no interest in the sport, so it was passed onto three-year-old Fernando, who loved the kart.

Before long, the youngster was excelling in the sport and beating most of the other children around homemade kart circuits, much to his father's delight. In 1988, at the age of just seven, he won all eight races in the Pola de Laviana Championship and took the title.

Unlike many child racers, Alonso also did well at school, so his mother was happy for him and his father to spend their weekends travelling from kart race to kart race. However, money was tight and it was essential to get some success so that he could be sponsored. Whether or not that spurred the boy on or not is unknown but, nevertheless, he won the Spanish Kart Championship in 1994, 1996 and 1997. And, more importantly, he was the World Junior Karting Champion in 1996.

At the age of 18, in 1999, Alonso competed in and won the Spanish Nissan Open Series, which quickly gained him a place in Formula 3000 for the following season. That year the newcomer impressed everyone by winning at Spa and, before long, he'd been snapped up to drive for the Minardi Formula One team in 2001. He was still only 20 years old and was the third-youngest Formula One driver in history when he debuted at the Australian Grand Prix. Despite putting in a good performance through the season, he failed to score any points in his first year.

BELOW
Alonso testing in Barcelona, Spain.

Alonso moved to Renault in 2002, where he spent the season as a test driver; time that was spent grooming him for his first season of racing with the team in 2003. And it was a good investment because, in his second race of 2003, he won the Hungarian Grand Prix, becoming the youngest driver ever to win a Formula One race. He finished the season in a worthy sixth place. The following year, he failed to win any races but nonetheless finished the Championship in fourth place.

However, that was all to change in 2005. Alonso stayed with Renault, driving alongside Italian, Giancarlo Fisichella. After finishing third in the first race of the season (in Australia) he won his next three Grands Prix, in Malaysia, Bahrain and Italy. It was a great start to the year and things continued to go well; Alonso also won at Monaco, the Nürburgring, France, Germany and China.

In between, he consistently achieved podium positions and had clinched the Drivers' Championship on points when he finished third in Brazil. At 24 years and 59 days old, Alonso was 18 months younger than the previous youngest Formula One champion, Emerson Fittipaldi.

By the end of the season, the young Spaniard helped Renault to win the Constructors' Championship for the first time.

LEFT
Alonso in action in his Renault at the Italian Grand Prix in Monza, 2005.

FAR LEFT
A frantic pitstop for Alonso at the Brazilian Grand Prix in 2005.

BELOW
Fernando Alonso celebrating winning the World Championship in Brazil, 2005.

Fernando Alonso has impressed the world of Formula One with his skill and determination at such a young age. Racing legend Niki Lauda said of him: "He's perfect, the most complete performer in Formula One today and thoroughly deserving of becoming the 2005 World Champion. Yet I also have to say that Alonso is extraordinary. The more pressure he has, the better he drives. I've never seen any driver of that age so completely composed and consistent. OK, so he made one slip at Montreal but, speaking for myself, I reckon that I would have made many more mistakes if I'd been in that position at that age. I can't find a single weakness in Alonso from any viewpoint. He's obviously a huge asset to the Renault team but more importantly a huge asset to the sport as a whole. I think he is perfect."

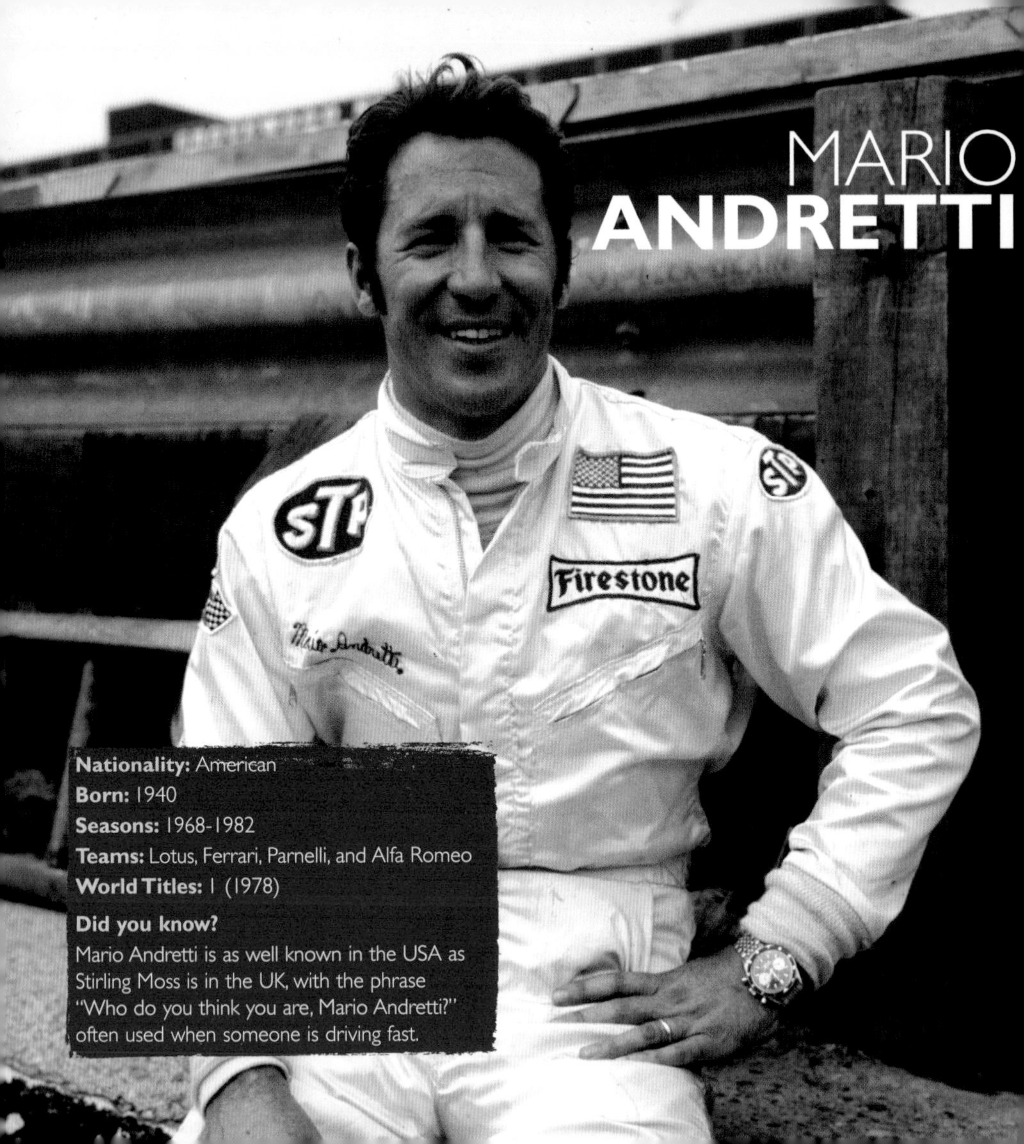

MARIO **ANDRETTI**

Nationality: American
Born: 1940
Seasons: 1968-1982
Teams: Lotus, Ferrari, Parnelli, and Alfa Romeo
World Titles: 1 (1978)

Did you know?
Mario Andretti is as well known in the USA as Stirling Moss is in the UK, with the phrase "Who do you think you are, Mario Andretti?" often used when someone is driving fast.

Mario Andretti is probably the most successful American racing driver of all time, and one of the few Americans to succeed in Formula One. He's also the only person to have won the Formula One World Championship, the Indianapolis 500 *and* the Daytona 500. Perhaps it's because he was born in Italy – a country that's passionate about motorsport.

It was in Italy that the 14-year-old Andretti first got a taste for motor racing, when he went to see the legendary Albert Ascari compete in the Italian Grand Prix at Monza. The following year Andretti's family emigrated to the USA and settled in Pennsylvania. There, he and his twin brother, Aldo, soon took to racing an old Hudson around dirt tracks. An accident and a badly injured arm put paid to Aldo's racing career (some have said that he would have been an even better driver), but Mario went on to compete in USAC sprint car and Indy car racing. In 1965 he entered the Indianapolis 500 and came third, taking the Rookie of the Year award (he went on to win the event in 1969; the first of four times).

Andretti had become an established racing driver in the USA, but he wanted to be successful in the more international Formula One. Lotus team owner, Colin Chapman, had spotted Andretti's talents and had promised him a drive in one of his cars whenever he liked so, in 1968, Andretti entered his first Grand Prix, at America's Watkins Glen. Driving a Lotus 49B, he took pole position but had to retire from the race itself due to mechanical problems.

Andretti raced sporadically in Formula One for the next few years, winning his first race with a Ferrari in 1971, in South Africa, and also racing for the Parnelli team. However, he was continuing to compete in USAC events, and travelling back and forth on Concorde, so he was unable to devote himself fully to Formula One until 1976. Now back with Lotus, Andretti really started to prove himself,

BELOW
Andretti driving in the 1990 Long Beach Grand Prix.

especially with the controversial ground-effect Lotus 78 and 79 cars. In 1978 he claimed the World Championship, after winning six races that season in a Lotus 79. His victory, however, was marred by the death of his friend and teammate, Ronnie Peterson, who was fatally injured in a crash at Monza.

Andretti and the Lotus team were unable to repeat their success and he had little luck over the next three seasons. He raced with Alfa Romeo in 1981 but returned to Ferrari at the end of the 1982 season and at Monza, just like at his Formula One debut, he took pole position – a fitting way to bow out of Formula One.

However, despite no longer competing in Formula One, Andretti continued to be a big name in North America, competing in Champ Car racing – racing for actor Paul Newman's team – and he won that Championship a total of four times.

In between all his other racing activities, Andretti competed many times at Le Mans, continuing even when he was in his 50s. Always desperate to win, his best performance was in 1995, when he finished second in a Porsche 956, driving with his son, Michael.

LEFT
Andretti at speed during the 1978 British Grand Prix.

FAR LEFT
Mario Andretti at his induction into the Automotive Hall of Fame in 2005.

BELOW
Mario Andretti (right) with his son Michael (left) and grandson Marco (centre), who have both followed a career in racing.

Michael is one of a number of Andretti family members who have gone into motorsport, and was a successful Indy car driver before setting up a number of car-related businesses. His teenage son – Mario's grandson – Marco Andretti is busy making a name for himself in American open-wheel racing. Meanwhile, Mario's youngest son, Jeff, has enjoyed a career driving Champ Cars. What's more, Mario's nephew, John – who is the son of his twin brother, Aldo – has been successful in a range of motorsport events, including competing seven times in the Indianapolis 500.

It must be the Italian blood!

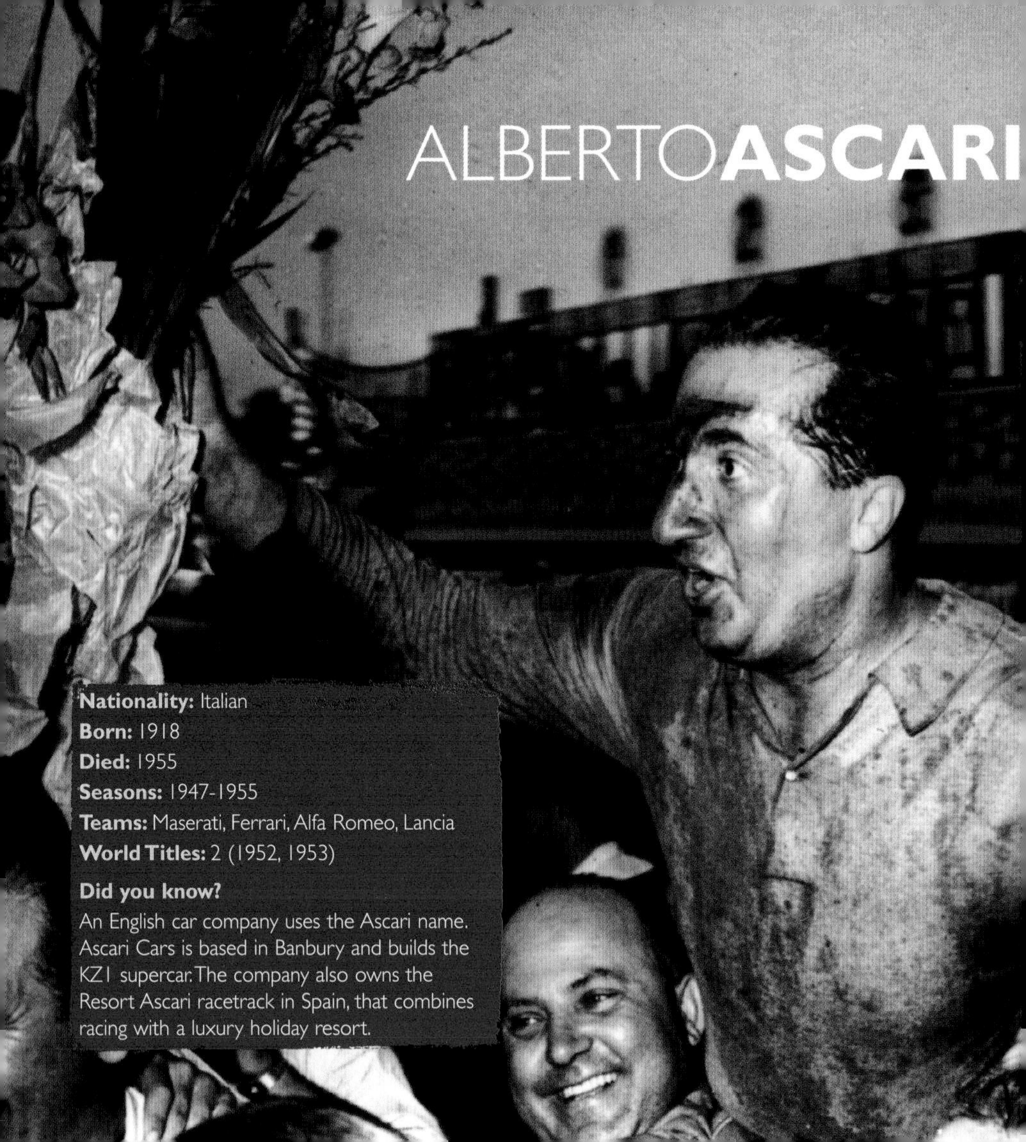

ALBERTO**ASCARI**

Nationality: Italian
Born: 1918
Died: 1955
Seasons: 1947-1955
Teams: Maserati, Ferrari, Alfa Romeo, Lancia
World Titles: 2 (1952, 1953)

Did you know?
An English car company uses the Ascari name. Ascari Cars is based in Banbury and builds the KZ1 supercar. The company also owns the Resort Ascari racetrack in Spain, that combines racing with a luxury holiday resort.

Alberto Ascari was destined to follow in the footsteps of his father, Alberto, who was a talented Grand Prix driver. Sadly, Ascari senior was killed in 1925 when his Alfa Romeo crashed at the French Grand Prix. His son was just seven years old when his father died but, in his short life, he'd been constantly exposed to the world of motor racing and the tragedy did nothing to put him off.

Indeed, he was so determined to follow in his father's footsteps that he twice ran away from school, and bought a motorcycle at the first opportunity.

After racing motorcycles for some years, Ascari's first car race was the 1940 Mille Miglia, driving a Ferrari. Unfortunately, the Second World War meant that he had to put his career on hold but, in 1947, he started racing again. Together with his friend, Gigi Villoresi, Ascari bought a 3CLT Maserati and started racing it on the circuits of northern Italy. He won the 1948 San Remo Grand Prix in the Maserati.

Enzo Ferrari, who'd been a close friend of Antonio Ascari, followed Ascari's development with interest and, in 1949, signed both him and Villoresi to the Ferrari team.

The year 1950 marked the start of Formula One racing and Ferrari made its debut at Monte Carlo, with Ascari and Villoresi on the team, along with Frenchman, Raymond Sommer. Ascari finished second in this event, and ended the season in fifth place in the Championship. The next year, he achieved two wins; at the Nürburgring and at Monza.

In those days, the American Indianapolis 500 was part of the Formula One circuit and in 1952 Ferrari sent Ascari across the Atlantic to be the only European driver to race there in the circuit's 11 years as a Formula One host. Sadly, he failed to finish that race but – amazingly – it was the only Grand Prix which he didn't win that season. The Italian dominated all six European races, setting new lap times for each circuit. He walked away with the Drivers' Championship, and did so again in 1953.

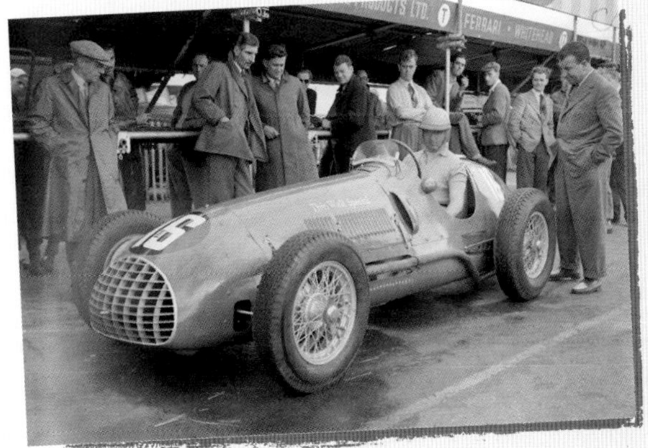

BELOW
Ascari in the pits at Silverstone in 1950.

Ascari had an unusual driving technique and never appeared relaxed behind the wheel. With his mouth set and his eyes concentrated, he seemed to whip his car along as his sensitive hands constantly manipulated the steering wheel. When he was really in a hurry, he took bends in a series of dicey jerks, rather than in one controlled slide.

Oddly, Ascari seemed to drive at his best when he was leading – it was almost as if he was scared to let anyone pass him. Indeed, it proved almost impossible for other drivers to overtake him in such situations. When he was further back in a race, though, Ascari didn't seem to push himself as hard.

Perhaps that was the reason that Ascari had less success in 1954, when he failed to finish a Formula One race. That said, he did win the Mille Miglia that year.

The 1955 season began in a similar vein, with Ascari retiring from the first two races, the second after he spectacularly crashed into the harbour after missing a chicane. He was pushing hard to beat Stirling Moss at the time, but didn't know that the Englishman was out of the race due to engine failure. The car sank into the

bubbling water and, after a few tense seconds, the crowd saw Ascari's pale-blue helmet bob to the surface and he was hauled into a nearby boat.

A week later, on 26th May, Ascari was at Monza and decided to do a few fun laps in a Sports Ferrari that belonged to his friend, Eugenio Castellotti, before lunch. Dressed in his ordinary clothes, and wearing Castellotti's helmet, he roared off. On the third lap, for reasons that have never been explained, the car skidded coming out of a bend, turned on its nose and somersaulted twice. Ascari was thrown out onto the track and died of multiple injuries a few minutes later.

Like his father, Alberto Ascari was killed doing what he loved best, but his full potential was perhaps never realised.

ABOVE
Ascari driving his Ferrari at Silverstone, 1950.

FAR LEFT
Ascari (right) chatting to Enzo Ferrari at the 1950 Italian Grand Prix.

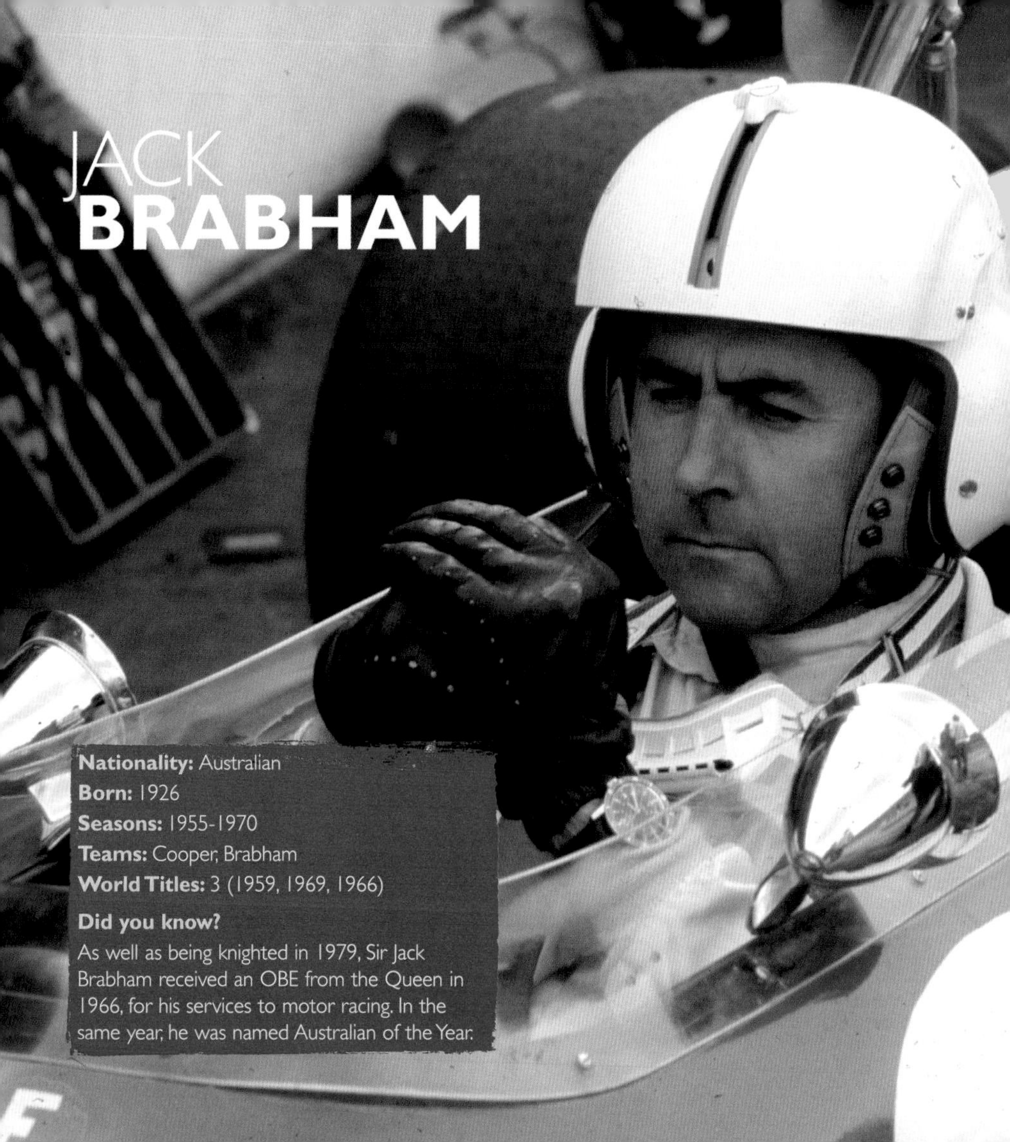

JACK **BRABHAM**

Nationality: Australian

Born: 1926

Seasons: 1955-1970

Teams: Cooper, Brabham

World Titles: 3 (1959, 1969, 1966)

Did you know?

As well as being knighted in 1979, Sir Jack Brabham received an OBE from the Queen in 1966, for his services to motor racing. In the same year, he was named Australian of the Year.

Australian Jack Brabham won the World Championship three times – the third time in a car bearing his own team's name. It was quite an achievement for the son of a Sydney grocer. Brabham's father was a keen motorist and taught Jack to drive a car when he was just 12 years old. He left school at the age of 15 and got a job at a garage, helping repair cars. Keen to get ahead in his chosen profession, the teenager spent his evenings studying engineering at college.

After serving in the airforce during the war, Brabham returned home and started his own car repair business. One of his customers was an American, Johnny Schonberg, who raced Midgets. Brabham helped to prepare his car for him but Schonberg's wife persuaded her husband to give up racing, and Brabham found himself with a car. So he decided to try his hand at racing.

Amazingly, despite being inexperienced, Brabham won the New South Wales Championship in his first season! Significantly, at this time he met up with engineer Ron Tauranac, who was to become a long-term friend and colleague.

Keen to pursue a career in racing, Brabham moved to England in 1955 and made his Grand Prix debut at Aintree, driving his own Maserati 250F. Before long, though, he joined the Cooper team, which was pioneering rear-engined cars in Formula One. Brabham quickly proved himself as a staggeringly competent driver, winning the Drivers' Championship in 1959 and 1960. In 1961, he took one of the mid-engined Coopers to the American Indianapolis 500 race, where the locals were stunned by the capabilities of this lightweight car, compared to their larger, front-engined machines.

As good as the Coopers were, Brabham decided to strike out on his own and, in 1961, he teamed up with his friend, Ron Tauranac, to found the Brabham Racing Organisation. Unfortunately, Formula One had introduced a 1500cc limit on engine size at this time, which did not suit

BELOW
Brabham at speed in a Brabham Repco car at Silverstone in 1966.

Brabham's aggressive driving style, and he failed to win any races with the new, less powerful cars. However, teammate Dan Gurney, from the USA, gave the Brabham team its first victory at Rouen in 1964.

Brabham's luck changed in 1966, when the allowed engine size of Formula One cars increased to a worthwhile 3000cc. He sourced a suitable engine from the Australian Repco company and, in its first year, the new car took Brabham to victory at the French, British, Dutch and German Grands Prix, allowing him to claim the Drivers' Championship with ease. He was the first Formula One driver to win the Championship in a car bearing his own name. The following year saw further success for the Brabham team, although this time it was driver Denny Hulme who took the Cup.

Brabham planned to retire from racing in 1970, but he couldn't sign a suitable driver to take his place, so he took it on himself to pilot a Brabham car once again. He started the season well with a win at the opening South African Grand Prix and announced his retirement after the Mexican Grand Prix.

Not only did he stop racing, but Brabham also sold his interest in the Brabham Racing Organisation to his partner, Ron Tauranac. Tauranac subsequently sold up to Formula One boss, Bernie Ecclestone, in 1972. The team then had some success with the likes of Graham Hill, Niki Lauda and Nelson Piquet, but it finally closed down in 1992.

Jack Brabham, meanwhile, returned to a quiet life in Australia, where he continued to run his garage business and made appearances at historical motorsport events. He was knighted in 1979 and all three of his sons have been involved in motorsport. His eldest, Geoff, has been particularly successful with his career in America. Most notably, he won the Le Mans 24 Hour race in 1991.

However, it is the name Jack Brabham which will be forever linked with Formula One, perhaps as much for the team as for his not inconsiderable driving skills.

ABOVE

Brabham takes the checkered flag to win the British Grand Prix at Aintree, 1955.

FAR LEFT

You wouldn't get today's F1 drivers doing this! Brabham checking his own tyres at Crystal Palace in 1969.

JENSON**BUTTON**

Nationality: British

Born: 1980

Seasons: 2000-

Teams: Williams, Benetton/Renault F1, BAR Honda

Did you know?

Jenson Button was engaged to Louise Griffiths, who appeared in the *Fame Academy* reality TV show. However, he left her in 2005, three months before they were due to be married.

enson Button was just 20 years old when he first raced a Formula One car. Frank Williams spotted his talent and, the previous year, had tried him out as a test driver and he turned out to be better than William's second driver, Bruno Junqueria, so Williams took him on as the team's second driver for the 2000 season.

Signing for Williams was the culmination of a childhood devoted to racing. Button began karting at the age of eight and was soon hooked. With the support of his father, John (himself a respected rallycross driver), the youngster excelled at the 1991 British Cadet Kart Championship, when he won all 34 races to take the Championship.

The talented lad continued to be a force to be reckoned in the karting world, at British, European and World stages. He was three times British Open Kart Champion and, in 1995, he won the Italian ICA Senior title. And, two years later, he became the youngest ever winner of the European Supercup A. He crowned his karting career later the same year by winning the Ayrton Senna Memorial Cup in Japan.

In 1998, Button moved from karts to cars, and drove for Haywood Racing in Formula Ford. That year he took the British Championship with nine wins, was runner-up in the European Championship and won the Formula Ford Festival. Not a bad first year, and one that led him to winning the McLaren Autosport BRDC Young Driver of the Year award.

The following year saw Button move up to Formula Three where, once again, he made an instant impression. Indeed, he took pole position for the very first race of the year. He finished the season with three wins under his belt and was third in the Championship; achievements that earned him the Avon Formula Three Rookie of the Year award.

It was in 1999 that Button had his first taste of a Formula One car, when he sampled a McLaren. He later tested for the Prost team and outpaced Jean Alesi! No wonder Williams signed him for the following season, to drive alongside Ralf Schumacher.

BELOW

You can't deny that F1 drivers are well treated. This is Button inside his motorhome during testing in 2004.

Button's first year in Formula One was a success, with him winning a point at his second Grand Prix, in Brazil, where he was the youngest ever British driver to score a World Championship point. He went on to finish the season in eighth place in the Drivers' Championship – an impressive result for a newcomer.

In 2001, Button moved to the Benetton team, where he struggled with an innovative new car. However, the following season, with the team renamed Renault F1, things improved and he finished the Championship in seventh place after consistently scoring points throughout the season.

Button was replaced by Fernando Alonso at Renault, so he went on to drive for BAR Honda in 2003, alongside Jacques Villeneuve, with whom Button fell out with in the first race of the season. Villeneuve spoilt a points-finish by coming into the pits when it was Button's turn. Even so, Button still finished ninth in the Championship that year.

In 2004, his second year with BAR Honda, despite not winning a race, Button managed to finish third in the Drivers' Championship, beaten only by the Ferrari

drivers. He achieved this by consistent point scoring, including four second places and six third places.

Sadly, he did less well in 2005, finishing ninth in the Championship, just one point behind his teammate, Rubens Barrichello. This was due in part to a disqualification at San Marino, which led to a three-race ban.

For 2006, Button signed a contract to drive for Williams, but backed out of it when he found that BMW would not be supplying engines to the team. Therefore, he remained with BAR Honda, after that team bought out his contract for a reputed $30-million. Ironically, though, Button had tried to return to Williams for 2005, but BAR Honda refused to let him go.

Despite his success on points, Jenson Button has yet to win a Formula One race and is still desperate to win the Drivers' Championship.

ABOVE
Button in action at the San Marino Grand Prix, 2006.

FAR LEFT
Jenson Button happy to have Pole Position in the Canadian Grand Prix, 2005.

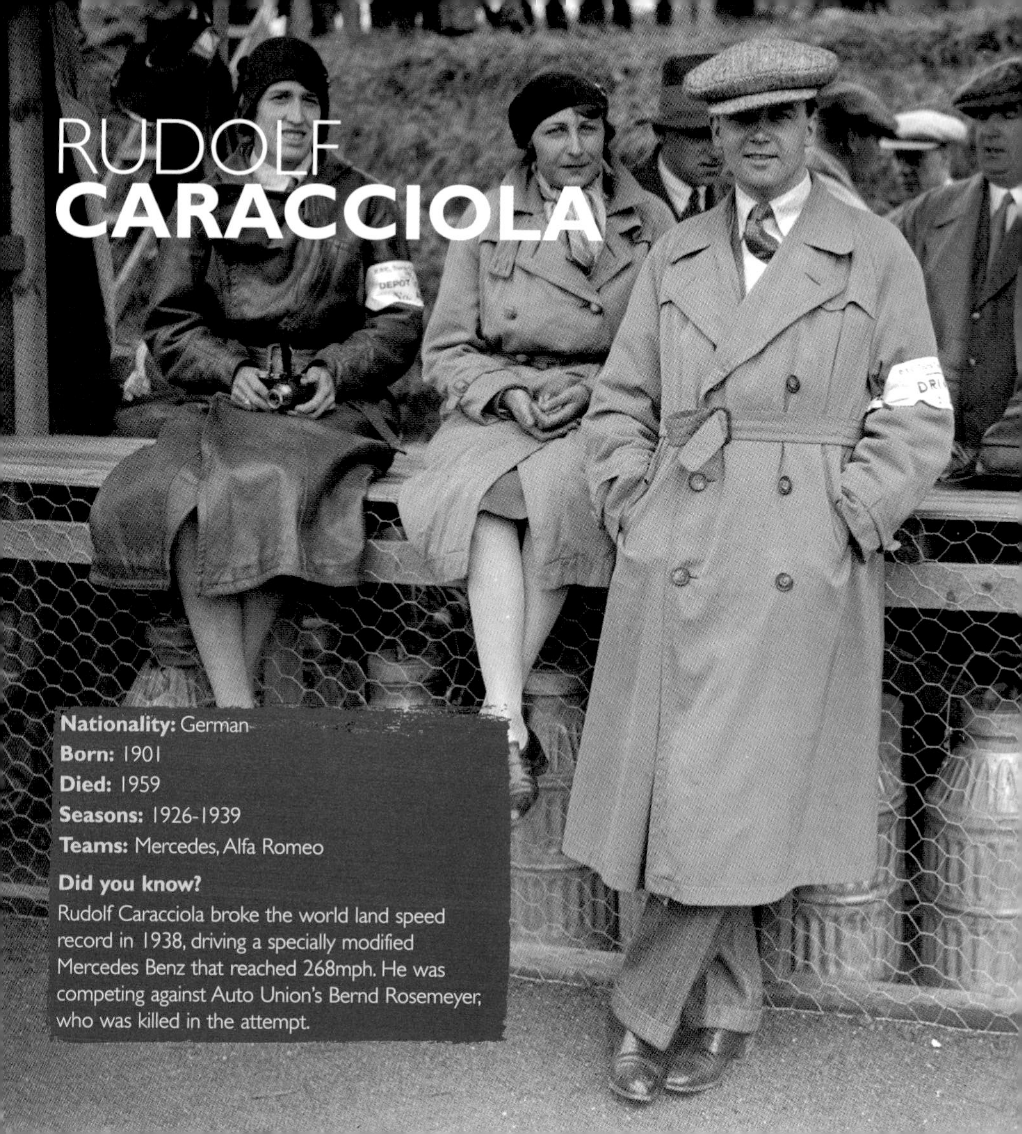

RUDOLF CARACCIOLA

Nationality: German
Born: 1901
Died: 1959
Seasons: 1926-1939
Teams: Mercedes, Alfa Romeo

Did you know?

Rudolf Caracciola broke the world land speed record in 1938, driving a specially modified Mercedes Benz that reached 268mph. He was competing against Auto Union's Bernd Rosemeyer, who was killed in the attempt.

Mercedes team manager, Alfred Neubauer, claimed that Rudolf Caracciola was "the greatest of all the great drivers." Praise, indeed, from a man who had worked with some of the most famous names in pre-war racing. Caracciola was thought by many people to be Italian, on account of his name. He was, though, born in Germany, albeit of Italian parents. His race career began as a weekend hobby, driving a Daimler-Benz lent to him by the car company, where he worked as a salesman.

He won his first race at the age of 22 and, after much pestering, managed to persuade his manager to lend him a Mercedes racecar with which to compete at the German Grand Prix. The deal was that the young man would race under his own name and not part of the Mercedes team. Unfortunately, the enthusiastic driver got off to a bad start, stalling on the start line. After a frantic push from his mechanic, he was away – in last place behind no less than 43 other cars.

Not to be deterred, Caracciola pressed on, in increasingly wet conditions. Other cars were losing control in the rain, and one span off and killed a spectator. Caracciola pressed on regardless and, amazingly, took the lead. It wasn't to last, though, as his engine developed a misfire and he had to pull into the pits to try to put it right. After cleaning all eight spark plugs himself, he was back in the race, and pushed on, desperate to prove his worth to the factory. After driving for 243 exhausting miles, Caracciola crossed the finishing line, totally unaware that he'd won the race – not only his first Grand Prix, but the first German Grand Prix, too. Never before or since has there been such an audacious start to a racing career.

Caracciola was soon nicknamed 'Reinmeister' (rain master) by his German fans, as he showed his prowess in the wet, time after time. His secret was in his smooth and calm driving style, plus a respect for the wet road surface. One of his most dramatic races was at the Tourist Trophy in Northern Island in 1929. Up

BELOW
Rudolf Caracciola on his way to winning the Irish International Grand Prix in 1933.

against some of Britain's finest drivers, he worked his way up from being five laps behind to winning the 30-lap race – again, in heavy rain. Two years later, he became the first non-Italian to win the Mille Miglia, driving a Mercedes Benz SSKL – maybe his ancestry had something to do with that triumph!

For the 1932 season, Caracciola moved to Alfa Romeo but was badly injured during practice at Monaco in 1933. This left him with a leg wound that never properly healed and he was to struggle with pain and a limp for the rest of his life.

In 1935, Caracciola suffered the loss of his wife in an avalanche in Switzerland, but he pushed on with his racing career and became European Champion that year, after returning to the Mercedes team. His most impressive performance of the season was at the Spanish Grand Prix. In those days, positions on the grid were determined by the simple expedient of drawing lots – and Caracciola chose the short straw that day. Starting from the very back

of the grid, he confused the accelerator and brake pedals (they varied from car to car) nd found himself speeding past the other astonished drivers, finally taking – and holding – the lead.

Caracciola went on to win the European Championship again in 1938 and 1939, before the Second World War put paid to his racing. After the war, Caracciola attempted o resume his career, but crashed in practice for the Indianapolis 500. His last success was t the 1952 Mille Miglia, where he came fourth in a Mercedes Benz 300SL.

Rudolf Caracciola died of a bone disease in 1959, aged just 58. He is remembered as one of the greatest pre-war racing drivers – if not one of the greatest of all time.

ABOVE

Caracciola in the rain at the 1930 Ulster Tourist Trophy race.

FAR LEFT

Rudolf Caracciola relaxing on the second day of the 1930 Irish Grand Prix in Dublin.

JIM CLARK

Nationality: British
Born: 1936
Died: 1968
Seasons: 1960-1968
Teams: Lotus
World Titles: 2 (1963, 1965)

Did you know?

The Jim Clarke Room is a small museum in Duns, Berwickshire, devoted to the life of the legendary driver. It includes trophies, photographs, model cars and other memorabilia.

Jim Clark was only 32 years old when he was killed in a motor-racing accident. However, he is still remembered as one of the greatest and best-loved drivers ever. Clark grew up on a farm in Scotland and enjoyed racing bicycles and, later, cars from an early age. His first competition driving was in rallying and local racing. He initially raced in his own Sunbeam Talbot, but scored his first big win in 1957 in a friend's Porsche 356 1600 Super, when he took the Border Motor Racing Club Trophy. Clark also hillclimbed a Triumph TR3 with some success at this time.

Before long, the young Scotsman was driving a Jaguar D-Tyre for the Borders Reivers Team and making a name for himself in England and Europe.

In 1958, Clark raced a Lotus Elite at Brands Hatch and was beaten only by Lotus's boss, Colin Chapman. Chapman was impressed by the young upstart and, the following year, Clark tested a Lotus Formula Two car and returned times comparable to the team's Formula One driver, Graham Hill, despite not having had any experience with single-seaters.

Chapman signed Clark to drive in his Formula Two team but, within months, he'd been switched to Formula One, Graham Hill having moved to BRM. Clark soon began to make a name for himself, scoring points at his second Grand Prix, at Spa, by finishing fifth. Sadly, this success was marred by a crash that claimed the life of his teammate, Alan Stacey.

At the end of the 1960 season, Louis Stanley, husband of BRM co-owner Jean Stanley, claimed that Clark "had a tendency to drive a fraction beyond his ability, and that fearlessness could be his undoing. If luck remains on his side, Clark will be a great asset to the Lotus team." In the event, Clark was to stay with Lotus throughout his career.

The 1961 season was a difficult one for Clark. A collision with a Ferrari driven by Wolfgang von Trip at the Italian Grand Prix led to the Ferrari careering into the crowd, killing the driver and 14 spectators.

BELOW
Clark in his Lotus, eyeing up the celebratory champagne before the 1965 British Grand Prix at Brands Hatch.

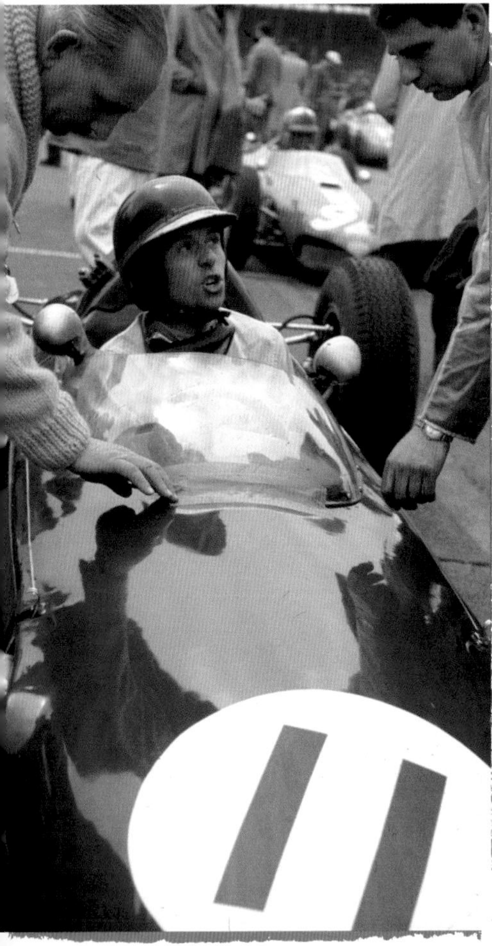

Although Clark knew the accident wasn't his fault, he still had to be involved in a lengthy enquiry afterwards.

The following year was a better one, with Clarke finishing second in the World Championship, despite having to deal with a number of mechanical problems with the new Lotus 25. However, 1963 was to be the year that Clarke first really excelled. With no less than seven wins, a second and a third place (out of a total of just 10 races), he won the World Championship with 54 points. He took his victory seriously, saying it gave him a responsibility to further the sport and take part in various social commitments. Although he admitted that he liked to return to the family farm in Scotland whenever possible, for a change of scene.

In 1965, Clark again won the World Championship, despite missing the Monte Carlo Grand Prix to travel to the US to compete in at the Indianapolis 500. Here, he was the first driver to win the race in a mid-engined car, and the only driver ever to win both events in the same year. He also won numerous other races of various types in 1965, including the Sebring Three-Hour Touring Car Race in a Lotus Cortina. There was no holding the man back and he was heralded by the British media as the new Stirling Moss.

Sadly, the following year was less successful, with Lotus struggling to compete with new 3.0-litre regulations, which it was ill-prepared for. With an underpowered car, Clark finished the Championship in sixth place.

For 1967, though, Lotus teamed up with Ford and Cosworth and was determined to fight back. The combination of the Lotus 49 car and Cosworth 3.0-litre V8 was destined to be a success, despite some initial mechanical problems. Graham Hill had returned to Lotus as Clark's teammate that year and the two became great friends. Clark took third place in the Championship.

The next year, 1968, began with Clark winning his 25th Formula One race and it looked as if victory would be in his grasp. However, it was not to be. Against his wishes, Clark travelled to Hockenheim to compete in a Formula Two race for Lotus on 7th April. The track was damp and, during testing, his car went off the track and hit some trees at a speed of over 240mph. Clark was killed instantly. It was claimed that the accident was due to a flat tyre, not driver error.

Jim Clarke's death shocked the motor-racing world and made front-page news the world over. He was not only a highly talented driver who could turn his hand to any form of motor racing, he was also – and perhaps more importantly – modest and a true sportsman.

ABOVE

A dramatic shot of Clark winning the 1963 British Grand Prix at Silverstone.

FAR LEFT

Clark talking to Lotus mechanics in the pits before a race in the mid 1960s.

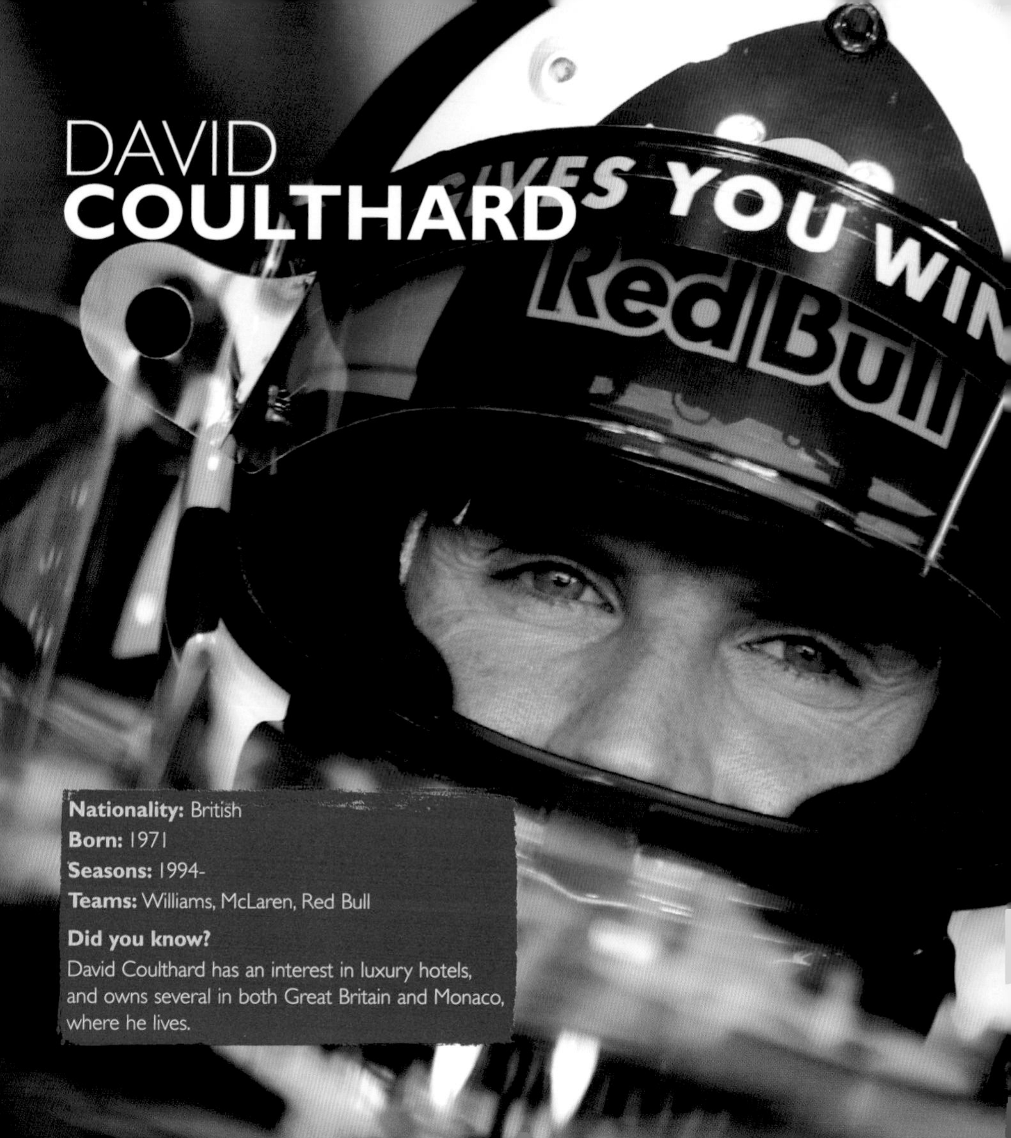

DAVID **COULTHARD**

Nationality: British

Born: 1971

Seasons: 1994-

Teams: Williams, McLaren, Red Bull

Did you know?

David Coulthard has an interest in luxury hotels, and owns several in both Great Britain and Monaco, where he lives.

David Coulthard followed in the footsteps of Innes Ireland, Jim Clarke and Jackie Stewart, in being a successful Scottish Formula One driver. He was brought up in Twynholm, a tiny village in the southwest of Scotland, where his father ran the family haulage company (which is now looked after by David's older brother, Duncan).

David's father, Duncan, was a keen karter and the young lad took up the same interest at an early age. His first race was at Larkhill, Strathclyde, where a fellow karter, Brian Smith, helped him with braking points by placing a crisp packet at the precise point he wanted Coulthard to apply his brakes. The boy followed the instructions to the tee and was soon on the road to karting success. In fact, at the age of just 12, he was the Scottish Junior Kart Champion, and he was to take this title again for the next five years running. What's more, in 1986 and 1987, he was also British Super Kart 1 Champion. The boy obviously had talent!

So much talent, in fact, that by 1989, at the age of just 18, he was racing in Formula Ford, where he won both the Dunlop/Autosport and P&O Ferries Junior Championships in his first year, which in turn led to him receiving the McLaren/Autosport Young Driver of the Year Award.

The following season, the young Coulthard moved to Paul Stewart Racing to compete in Formula Vauxhall Lotus and the GM Lotus Euroseries. He came a respectable fourth and fifth, respectively, in the Championships.

Staying with Paul Stewart, Coulthard progressed to British Formula 3 in 1991, and finished the season second in the Championship. In 1992 and 1993 he raced in Formula 3000, and came ninth and then third at the end of the seasons. In 1992, Coulthard also won the GT class at Le Mans, in a Jaguar.

While he was competing in Formula 3000, Coulthard tested for Benetton and Williams and, as a result, became Williams' test driver for the 1994 season. He was

BELOW

A young Coulthard celebrating his first Grand Prix victory at Portugal in 1995. With him are his parents and girlfriend, Andrea Murray.

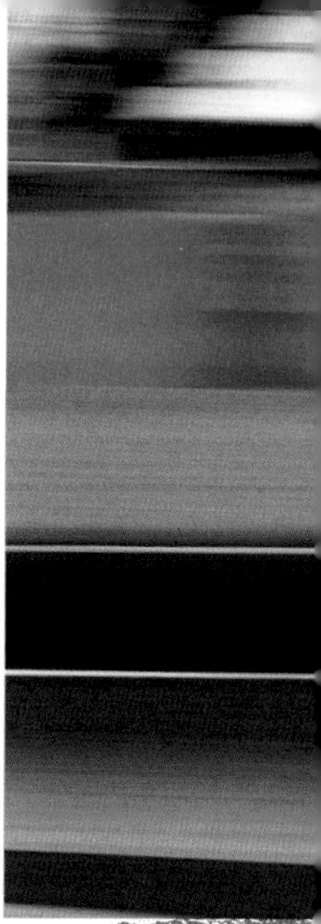

meant to continue in Formula 3000 that year but a tragic event intervened; Williams' driver Ayrton Senna was killed at the San Marino Grand Prix. Coulthard was called in to take Senna's place, alongside Damon Hill, and his Formula One career began in earnest.

Coulthard spent his first season very much in the shadow of Hill and, on four occasions, had to step aside to let ex-champion Nigel Mansell drive, because Williams wanted a big name in the car. Even so, the Scot drove well when the opportunities arose, and took second place at Estoril, and finished eighth in the Championship. His performance was enough to gain him the Scottish Sports Personality of the Year and ITV Young Sports Personality of the Year awards.

It was also good enough to gain him a full place on the Williams team in 1995, albeit still second to Damon Hill. Coulthard put in mixed performances, with a win at Portugal tainted by some mistakes in other races. Even so, he took third place in the Drivers' Championship.

Sadly, it was not good enough for Williams, who replaced him with Jacques Villeneuve for 1996.

Coulthard, meanwhile, moved to McLaren to partner Mika Häkkinen. At the end of an uneventful season, he took seventh place in the Championship. However, the following year he won two Grands Prix and finished the season in a respectable third place.

Coulthard stayed with McLaren and, in 1998, the team had the fastest cars on the track, but the Scot had to give way to his teammate Häkkinen, who went on to win the Championship. Coulthard made do with fourth place; a position he matched in 1999.

In 2001, Coulthard managed to finish the season in second place, beaten only by Michael Schumacher. After that, though, his performances were less successful and he left McLaren at the end of 2004.

His next team was the new Red Bull Racing, who were keen to have a big-name driver on their books, alongside the less well-known Christian Klien and Vitantonio Liuzzi.

Although a Championship win has so far eluded Coulthard, he is able to boast having the second-most race wins, beaten only by Michael Schumacher. And, as of 2005, he was also the highest-scoring British driver ever, with 483 points.

ABOVE

A dramatic image of David Couthard's McLaren during the 2002 French Grand Prix.

FAR LEFT

Coulthard in pensive mood at the 2005 Japanese Grand Prix in Suzuka.

JUAN-MANUEL **FANGIO**

Nationality: Argentinean
Born: 1911
Died: 1995
Seasons: 1949-1958
Teams: Alfa Romeo, Maserati, Mercedes, Ferrari
World Titles: 5 (1951, 1954, 1955, 1956, 1957)

Did you know?

Fangio was known as 'El Maestro' by his peers, a name reputedly given to him by Stirling Moss, but his fans affectionately called him 'Old Bandy Legs' on account of his stance.

Juan-Manuel Fangio is one of the greatest names in Formula One, yet this Argentinean legend didn't begin racing at Grand Prix level until he was 38 years old. The son of an Italian immigrant, he took part in his first car race at the age of 18, in a Ford taxi. Soon after, the young garage owner took part in long-distance races on South American dirt roads. And these really *were* long-distance events. For instance, Fangio won the Gran Premio del Norte in 1940 after racing for over 6000 miles from Buenos Aires to Lima and back again.

BELOW
A 1949 shot of Fangio piloting a Ferrari at Monza.

After World War II, Fangio was established as a talent in his own country and the government sponsored him to travel to Europe to develop his career and promote Argentina. After proving himself in a Maserati in 1949, he was recruited by Alfa Romeo for the 1950 season. That year, he came second in the Championship, but the following year he won it for the first of five times.

For the 1952 season, Fangio moved to Maserati and started the season well. Then he had to travel from to Monza in Italy to compete in a race. He ended up driving overnight from Paris, after missing his flight, and arrived at the circuit just half an hour before the start of the race. Relegated to the back of the grid, Fangio struggled to improve his position and pushed his Maserati too hard and it went into a slide. His reactions slowed due to his lack of sleep, the normally superb driver was unable to regain control and the car hit bank and somersaulted through the air, throwing Fangio out, almost killing him. His neck was broken in the accident and he was unable to race again that year.

However, Fangio was back in action for 1953, still driving for Maserati, and finished the Championship in second place. The wily Argentinean always ensured that the team's mechanics were on his side, by giving them 10 percent of his winnings. After complaining about a bad vibration on his car during practice at the Italian Grand Prix that year, Fangio was pleased to

find that the problem had been solved by race day. However, all the mechanics had done was swapped Fangio's car for that of his teammate!

1954 saw Fangio switch allegiance, mid-season, to the Mercedes team and he won six out of eight Grand Prix races, taking the Championship with ease. He repeated his success in 1955, driving the legendary Mercedes W196 Monoposto, along with teammate Stirling Moss. At the end of the season, Mercedes had won, not only in Formula One, but in many other major Championships too. However, after a Mercedes 300SLR crashed at Le Mans in 1955, team boss, Alfred Neubauer, decided to withdraw the company from racing altogether.

Therefore, for 1956, he moved to Ferrari, replacing Alberto Ascari, who was killed at Monza the previous year. Once again, he took the Championship with ease, winning three races, and coming second in all the others.

Despite this success, Fangio returned to Maserati in 1957, when he had a magnificent win at the Nüburgring, in which he passed the two leading

Ferraris in his less powerful car. Indeed, he got past Mike Hawthorn by straight-lining through a final bend. No wonder Fangio was known as 'El Maestro'.

Fangio retired in 1958 and his last race was the French Grand Prix, where Mike Hawthorn slowed to let Fangio's Maserati finish before him, as a mark of respect to the Maestro. Fangio got out of his car in the pits and said simply, "It's finished".

He then returned to Argentina where he ran his own Mercedes dealership. He also acted as an ambassador for Mercedes and drove his old racecars in demonstration laps.

Juan-Manuel Fangio died in 1995 in Buenos Aires in 1995, at the age of 84, but he is remembered as one of the true great drivers; one who won 24 of the 51 races he competed in.

ABOVE
Fangio – a master in action at the 1957 Italian Grand Prix.

FAR LEFT
Fangio with his partner Andrea at Silverstone in 1954.

EMERSON**FITTIPALDI**

Nationality: Brazilian
Born: 1946
Seasons: 1970-1980
Teams: Lotus, McLaren, Fittipaldi
World Titles: 2 (1972, 1974)

Did you know?

In 2005, Emerson Fittipaldi became team principal for the Brazilian A1 Grand Prix team. This is a race series where drivers compete for their country, rather than for a private team. One of the drivers was Fittipaldi's nephew, Christian Fittipaldi.

Brazilian Champion Emerson Fittipaldi's parents both raced production cars after the Second World War, so it's perhaps not surprising that both he and his brother, Wilson, should have got involved in motor racing. Furthermore, their father – Wilson senior – was a well-known motorsport journalist and radio commentator.

Despite this family background, though, the brothers' parents wouldn't help to finance the boys' career in racing. Instead, the teenagers had to pay for it themselves, and they did this by setting up a custom-car spares business, which began with a steering wheel they made for their mother's car. The venture was a great success and the brothers went on to build and race their own karts, with Emerson becoming the Brazilian Kart Champion by the age of 18.

The next step was racing Volkswagen-powered Formula Vee single-seaters which, once again, the two built themselves. And, once again, Emerson proved himself the better driver and won the Championship in 1967. This success persuaded him to abandon his mechanical engineering course and travel to England. There, despite not speaking a word of English, he bought a Formula Ford car and was an immediate success on the track.

Before long, he'd moved to Formula Three, driving for the Jim Russell Driving School team, and continued to win races on a regular basis. He soon drew the attention of Lotus boss, Colin Chapman, who was looking for a new Formula One driver for the 1970 season.

Emerson made his Formula One debut in the 1970 British Grand Prix, and put in a good performance, followed by similar drives in Germany and Austria. Then came the ill-fated Italian Grand Prix at Monza, where teammate, Jochen Rindt, was killed in a practice accident. Earlier that day, Emerson had also crashed at high speed; he was shaken but unhurt. Lotus's other driver at the time, John Miles, was so affected by Rindt's death that he immediately retired from Formula One, leaving newcomer Fittipaldi in the unusual position of being

BELOW
Emerson Fittipaldi driving his Lotus to victory at the British Grand Prix at Brands Hatch in 1972.

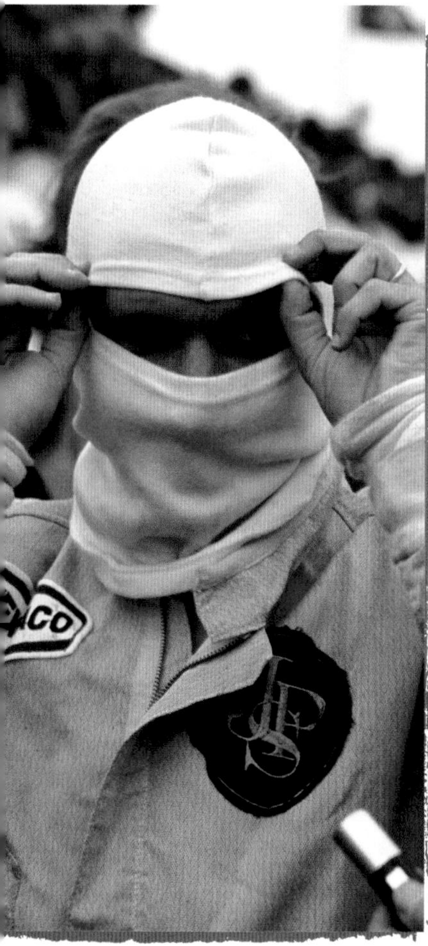

team leader, after only racing in three Grands Prix.

He immediately rose to the challenge and won his next race, the USA Grand Prix at Watkins Glen. This ensured that Rindt won the Championship posthumously on points, which went some way to lift the team's spirits.

The next year, 1971, was a disappointment because Fittipaldi had been badly injured in a road-car accident in France, which affected him both physically and mentally. However, he was back on form in 1972 with the superb Lotus 72 car. He won five of the 12 races that year, securing the Constructors' Championship for Lotus and making himself World Champion at the age of just 25; at the time, the youngest driver ever.

Lotus picked up the Constructors' Championship again the following year, but this time Fittipaldi was beaten by Jackie Stewart in the Drivers' Championship.

Fittipaldi then left Lotus to drive for McLaren in 1974, and that year he won three races and clinched the Championship for a second time. He did almost as well the following year, too, but after a great year he had to make do with second place, behind Ferrari's Niki Lauda.

It seemed that Fittipaldi was on a roll with McLaren, so it was a shock to his fans when he announced that he was

ɛaving the team in favour of a small outfit run by his brother, Wilson. Sponsored by ɪrazil's state-owned sugar industry, the Fittipaldi team couldn't compete with the big layers, despite their lead driver's undoubted skills. Even so, loyalty to his family and ountry meant that Fittipaldi stayed with the team for five years, but the best result he ould manage in all that time was a second place.

Fittipaldi retired from driving in 1980, but stayed on to manage his team until it nally folded in 1982. He then returned to Brazil to manage the family's citrus farm and ar accessory business. However, by 1984 he was back behind the wheel of a racing car, nis time in the American CART series. Fittipaldi continued to compete until 1996 when e retired again after an accident.

Even that didn't stop him for long, though, because in 2005 he competed in the Grand rix Masters event in South Africa, where he finished second behind Nigel Mansell.

ABOVE

Emerson Fittipaldi sprints from the pits at the Indy Grand Prix in Surfer's Paradise Australia.

FAR LEFT

Fittipaldi adjusts his balaclava, while being interviewed, 1975.

MIKA HAKKINEN

Nationality: Finnish
Born: 1968
Seasons: 1991-2001
Teams: Lotus, McLaren
World Titles: 2 (1998, 1999)

Did you know?

Mika Häkkinen has many fans around the world, not least in his home country of Finland. His nicknames include the Flying Finn, Iceman and, in Finland, 'Häkä' which means carbon monoxide.

BELOW
Hakkinen in the pits at the 2000 Canadian Grand Prix in Montreal.

Mika Häkkinen, like most successful racing drivers, started off racing karts; in his case from the age of just five years old. He went on to win his first race when he was seven, and had won his first Championship by the time he was 11 years old. From then on, he went on to be Finnish Karting Champion no less than five times.

By the time the talented youngster was 19, it was time to move on from karts – and he did this in style. In his first year racing Formula Ford 1600 cars, he won the Finnish, Swedish and Nordic Championships. The following year, Häkkinen walked away with the Opel Lotus Euroseries Championship and the British GM Euroseries Championship. The next stage was Formula Three, and this new talent won the British Championship in 1990, his second year of entering.

With a background like this, what Formula One team wouldn't take notice? Häkkinen was signed by Lotus to race with them in 1991 but, unfortunately, the team was past its prime; the Finn gave his best performances, but the cars were simply not up to the challenge. Even so, in 1992, he finished a respectable eighth in the Championship.

Häkkinen wanted more, though, and moved to McLaren as a test driver, realising that this would give him a foothold to racing with a top team. He achieved this sooner than he expected, taking over from Michael Andretti mid-season. In qualifying for his first race, at Estoril, Häkkinen out-performed teammate Ayrton Senna, proving to the world that he was someone to watch out for.

The Finn was McLaren's team leader in 1994 and 1995, but he failed to win any races during these seasons. At the Australian Grand Prix in 1995, a tyre failure caused Häkkinen to crash into a wall and he needed an emergency tracheotomy to save his life.

Luckily, he made a full recovery for the 1996 season, and stayed with the now improving McLaren team. Again, though, he failed to win any races, but nonetheless finished sixth in the Championship; a

position he matched in 1997, when he was driving with David Coulthard. That year, he began winning races again, with a first in Australia and Spain.

Häkkinen and McLaren were on a roll – with Adrian Newey, the former Williams technical director, on board – and it showed in 1998. Häkkinen won no less than eight races that year and clinched the Drivers' Championship with ease, proving he was one man who could give Michael Schumacher a run for his money.

The following year, 1999, was less easy for Häkkinen, with the McLaren cars less reliable and Schumacher determined to fight back. The Finn struggled at the start of the season and lost points, but soon got back on form and was ahead of Schumacher on points by the time the German was injured at Silverstone and was out of the Championship Up against Ferrari's Eddie Irvine, the Championship went to the final race in Japan which Häkkinen managed to win and so claim the title for the second year in a row – something few drivers have done.

Eager to score a hat-trick in in 2000, Häkkinen fought hard throughout the season,

ut was pushed into second place by a determined Schumacher. Even so, he displayed ome inspired driving, especially at Spa, where he stormed to victory, overtaking both chumacher and Ricardo Zonta in one go.

The next year was to be Häkkinen's last season in Formula One, and he put in an mpressive performance once again, with wins at Silverstone and at Indianapolis. At the nd of the year, he said he was going to take a break from racing but, in mid-2003 he nnounced his full-time retirement. There were rumours of a comeback in 2005 and läkkinen was in talks with Williams but nothing came of it. Instead, he took up German ouring Car racing from 2005.

Whatever the future holds for Mika Häkkinen, it is unlikely that he will return to the port which made him famous, but he will always be remembered as one of the great ormula One drivers.

ABOVE

A win for Hakkinen at the 2001 British Grand Prix at Silverstone.

FAR LEFT

A delighted Hakkinen waving to the crowd after getting pole position for the 1998 Grand Prix at Silverstone.

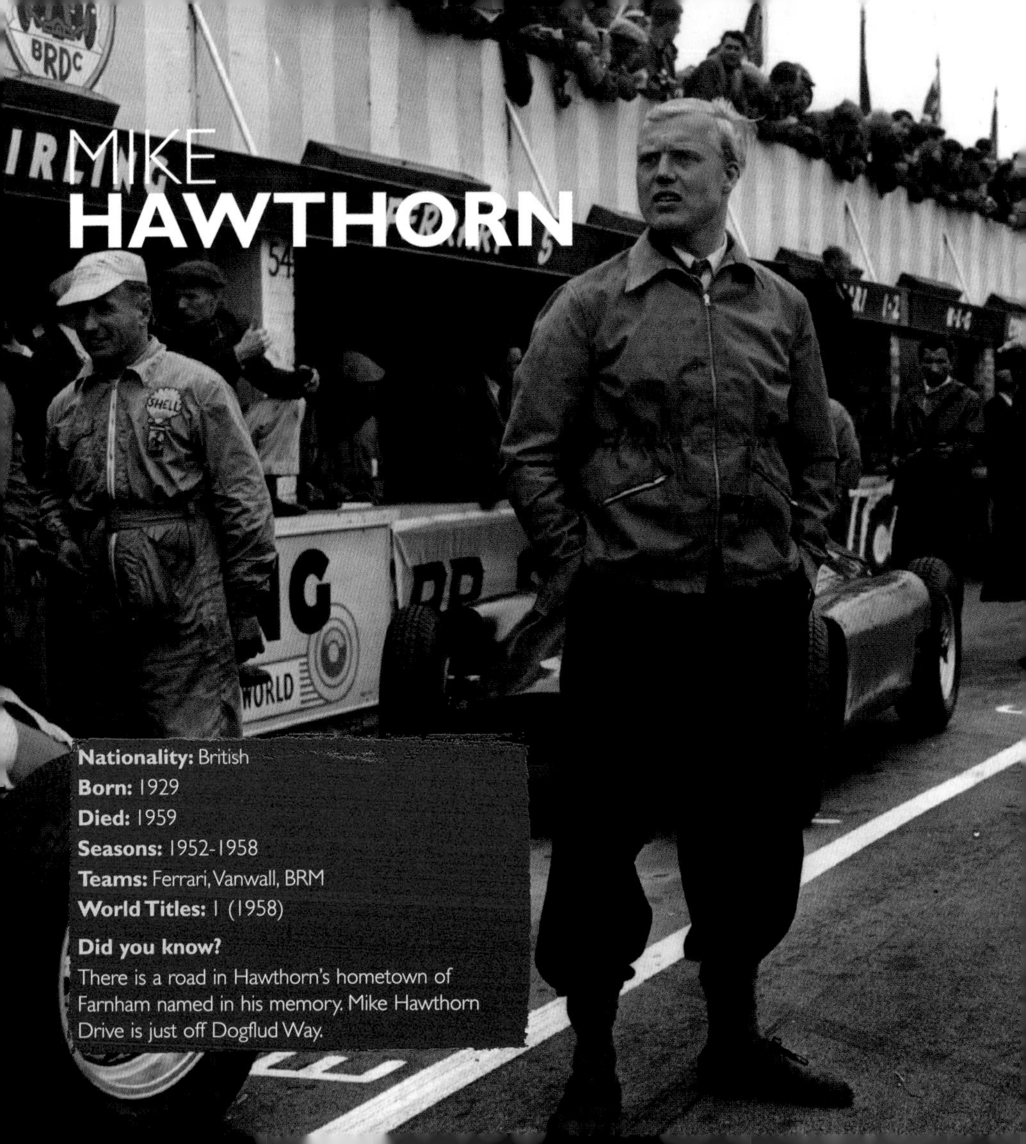

MIKE HAWTHORN

Nationality: British

Born: 1929

Died: 1959

Seasons: 1952-1958

Teams: Ferrari, Vanwall, BRM

World Titles: 1 (1958)

Did you know?

There is a road in Hawthorn's hometown of Farnham named in his memory. Mike Hawthorn Drive is just off Dogflud Way.

Vith his blonde hair and bowtie, Mike Hawthorn was a dashing English sportsman ᵛho lived life to the full. Who better to be the first-ever British World Champion? he young Hawthorn was brought up surrounded by cars and motorcycles. His ıther, Leslie, had raced motorcycles before the Second World War and also ran a arage business in Farnham, not far from the famous Brooklands circuit. By the age f nine, Hawthorn had made up his mind that his was going to be a racing driver, nd he spent all his spare time at Brooklands, dreaming of being on the circuit.

BELOW
Hawthorn concentrates hard as he negotiates a corner in his Ferrari at Silverstone, 1958.

His father, however, had more realistic dreams for his son, and sent him to public :hool followed by technical college. The boy then took an apprenticeship with a ɔmmercial vehicle manufacturer; the plan being that he'd eventually return to the family usiness and help build that up.

In the meantime, though, his father was happy to encourage his son's racing hobby, ıpplying him with motorcycles and then cars. And when he wasn't racing, the teenager ɔed around the countryside with his friends, going from pub to pub in search of beer nd girls.

Before long, his racing began to take over, as he quickly became established on the ub circuit, driving a Riley sports car, which his father bought for him in 1950. And ıen, in 1952, Hawthorn had a chance to race at Goodwood, in a Formula wo Cooper-Bristol which a family friend ad lent him. Up against the likes of Juan lanual Fangio, Hawthorn shocked veryone by winning the Formula Two ıce, plus the Formula Libre event, and ıen came second in the main race, for ormula One cars.

Inspired by his success, Hawthorn ecided to race the Cooper-Bristol in the :maining Formula One races of the :ason, which was dominated by Ferrari- riving Alberto Ascari. Wearing his ademark bowtie, Hawthorn finished ɔurth in Belgium and Holland, and third

in the UK, ranking him fourth in the Championship.

Enzo Ferrari was impressed by the newcomer's performance and promptly hired him for the 1953 season. Hawthorn's one win that year was at the French Grand Prix, at Reims, where he crossed the line just ahead of Fangio. On the podium afterwards, Hawthorn burst into tears when the National Anthem was played, and Fangio hugged him, saying he was a "nice young fellow". The French public also loved him, calling him Le Papillon, or The Butterfly, on account of his bowties. Back home, though, the tabloid press hounded him for his incessant partying and womanising. He was also accused of evading national service although, in truth, this was because of a kidney ailment.

The bad news continued in 1954, when Hawthorn was badly injured in a race in Sicily, and then his father was killed in a road accident. The high point of the year was a win at the Spanish Grand Prix.

Hawthorn then left Ferrari to drive the less successful Vanwell and then BRM teams. He made the headlines once again in 1955, when he won Le Mans in a Jaguar. This was the year that a Mercedes crashed into the crowds, killing over 80 people and Hawthorn was, for a while, blamed for the incident. He was eventually cleared, but the disaster weighed heavily on his mind.

He returned to Ferrari in 1957, when he became friends with teammate Peter Williams, another driver who enjoyed to party. Tragically, though, Williams was killed at the Nürburgring in 1958 and this was the final straw for Hawthorn; he was no longer interested in racing. Reluctantly, he completed the season and finished just one point in front of Stirling Moss, to become World Champion.

The triumph was mixed with the tragedy of the loss of his friend's life, though, and Hawthorn retired from racing and was looking forward to a quiet life with his fiancée, model Jean Howarth, and running the family business in Farnham.

Tragically, however, this was not to be. Hawthorn still enjoyed driving fast on public roads and, on 22nd January 1959, his Jaguar span in the wet on the Guildford bypass and the 29-year-old was dead. In the days that followed, thousand of people came to the crash site to pay their respects to this English hero.

ABOVE
Hawthorn taking the lead at the 1956 British Grand Prix at Silverstone.

FAR LEFT
Mike Hawthorn wearing his trademark bowtie at Silverstone in 1952.

DAMON **HILL**

Nationality: British
Born: 1960
Seasons: 1992-1999
Teams: Brabham, Williams, Arrows, Jordan
World Titles: 1 (1996)

Did you know?

Damon Hill is a keen guitarist, and has played with ex-Beatle George Harrison and heavy rockers Def Leppard. During his days with Jordan, he played alongside team boss and drummer, Eddie Jordan, at Silverstone parties.

The son of Formula One legend, Graham Hill, the young Damon Hill was brought up in the world of motorsport but, as a child, he complained that having to attend Grands Prix and mixing with stars to be "boring adult stuff". However, at the age of 11, Hill was in the paddock at Silverstone when he was offered a go on a 50cc Honda 'monkey' bike. The lad was so impressed, he persuaded his father to buy him a similar bike of his own.

By 1981, after the death of his father, Hill was dabbling in motorbike racing, while scraping together a living as a builder and despatch rider. His mother, though, wasn't impressed and decided to wean him off dangerous motorbikes by sending him to the Winfield Racing School at Magny-Cours, France, in 1983. Here he learnt to drive single-seater racing cars but stubbornly stuck to bike racing until the end of 1984. Then, Hill switched from bikes to Formula Ford and won his first race at Brands Hatch. His racing car career had begun in earnest.

Over the following years, he competed in Formula Ford and then Formula Three and Formula 3000. Despite proving himself as a talented driver, Hill didn't achieve any noteworthy victories during this time.

In 1991, Hill began working as a test driver for Williams, taking over from Mark Blundell, who'd moved on to racing-proper. Hill soon proved himself to be competent behind the wheel of a Formula One car and, the following season, he drove for the troubled Brabham team while, at the same time, continuing to test for Williams.

Keeping in with Williams proved a good move because Hill was asked to race with that team for 1993, in place of Nigel Mansell and alongside Alain Prost. It was a great year, in that Hill won three races and was runner up in four.

The 1994 season was marred by the death of Hill's new team-mate, Ayrton Senna, which led to him being the team

BELOW
Hill in action in a Honda during the German Grand Prix at Hockenheim in 1999.

leader, a position at which he excelled. By the last race of the season, at Adelaide, Hill had won six races and come second in five, putting him just one point behind Michael Schumacher. Beating the German in Australia would have clinched the Championship for Hill.

Sadly, though, it was not to be. Schumacher hit a wall and then knocked into Hill's car – some say deliberately – causing both drivers to have to retire. Schumacher subsequently walked away with the Championship, leaving Hill with second place. Still, he was presented with the BBC TV Sports Personality of the Year award that year.

Hill had to make do with second place – again behind Schumacher – in 1995, this time teamed with David Coulthard. The following year, though, Hill really excelled and won the Championship with Williams. He had no less than eight wins that year and, amazingly, started every race of the season on the front row of the grid.

In typical Williams style, however, Hill's contract was not renewed after he had won the Championship and – surprisingly, perhaps – he moved to the new Arrows team for 1997. Unfortunately, the cars didn't prove to be as good as Hill had expected and he spent the season plagued by mechanical problems. This was most apparent at the Hungarian Grand Prix, where Hill was on track to win when a 10p washer failed on his car and so he lost to team-mate Jacques Villeneuve.

Not impressed, Hill moved to Jordan for 1998, driving with Ralf Schumacher. Despite a bad start to the season – again, due

LEFT

Damon Hill F1 World Champion 1996.

FAR LEFT

The start of a career – six-year-old Damon Hill sitting in his father's Lotus at Silverstone.

BELOW

Damon Hill celebrates his racing career after his retirement in 1999.

o mechanical problems – Hill put in a good show and ave the team its first ever win, at Spa.

Hill stayed with Jordan for 1999 but the season didn't o well for him. After an unfortunate crash at Montreal nd a poor performance in France, he wanted to retire but is team persuaded him to see out the year. Clearly lemotivated, Hill finished the season a pale shadow of his ormer self, and some argued he should have retired the revious year.

Since retiring, Hill has spent time with his wife and amily, and has been involved in several business ventures, ncluding car dealerships and a high-performance car easing company.

To some, he is just the son of Graham Hill, but Damon vas a talented and successful driver in his own right, and hat is how he should be remembered.

GRAHAM **HILL**

Nationality: British
Born: 1929
Died: 1975
Seasons: 1958-1975
Teams: Lotus, BRM, Brabham, Hill
World Titles: 2 (1962, 1968)

Did you know?

Graham Hill's distinctive helmet design with its white stripes, was based on the insignia of London Rowing Club, of which he was a keen member. His son, Damon, carried on this tradition when he started racing.

BELOW

Hill concentrating during practice for the 1966 British Grand Prix at Brands Hatch.

Graham Hill did not even drive a car until he was 24 years old, yet went onto become a Formula One legend during the 1960s and 1970s, his dashing good looks and playboy lifestyle making him a media hero. Lack of money at a young age led to his delay in driving and, when Hill finally bought a car, it was an old Austin with failing brakes. To stop, he used to scrub the tyres against the kerb, and later claimed that this was essential training in becoming a racing driver: "The chief qualities of a racing driver are concentration, determination and anticipation," he claimed. "A 1929 Austin without brakes develops all three; anticipation rather more than the first two, perhaps."

That first car was paid for by his job at Smiths Instruments, and it was while he was working there that he heard about a new racing school at Brands Hatch, that offered people the chance to drive a Formula Three car for five shillings a lap. Hill did four laps and it changed his life for ever.

Before long, Hill had left Smiths and was working as a mechanic for a similar school. His talents as a driver were noted and, before long, he was competing in races and acting as an instructor. A chance meeting with Colin Chapman led to Hill working at Lotus as a mechanic for the princely sum of £1 a day.

He did some racing in Lotus's Formula Two cars, but Hill was convinced that he should be racing the cars, not maintaining them and, after much cajoling, he managed to persuade Chapman to promote him to full-time driver. And in 1958, he made his Formula One debut.

However, he became disillusioned with the Lotus's mechanical failures and so, in 1960, he moved to BRM and began to show real promise. Even so, it wasn't until 1962, when BRM had produced a new V8-engine car, that Hill began to win races, his first being at Zandvoort. By the end of the season, he was World Champion.

Sadly, mechanical problems meant he was unable to repeat his success with BRM, although he did win the Indianapolis 500 in 1966. By 1967 he had returned to Lotus where he teamed up with Jim Clark, with whom he became good friends.

After Clark's tragic death in 1968, Hill was determined to keep his friend's spirit alive and went on to win the Championship that year, clinching the title in the final round. He was approaching his 40th birthday at the time.

That, though, was the beginning of the end of Hill's Grand Prix career. He had limited success in 1969, despite a win at Monaco – his fifth at the notorious circuit. A bad crash at the US Grand Prix at Watkins Glen that year led to Hill being thrown from his Lotus 49B and his injuries meant that he was confined to a wheelchair for some time after, but returned to racing for the following season.

A brief spell with Brabham was unremarkable and then, in 1973, Hill set up his own racing team – Hill Embassy Racing – for which he also drove. Sadly, he and the team were unsuccessful

LEFT
Graham Hill wins in Monte Carlo, 1965.

FAR LEFT
Hill in his BRM before the start of a race, 1964.

BELOW
Two year old Damon, already showing signs of following in his father Graham Hill's footsteps.

and, after failing to qualify for the 1975 Monaco Grand Prix, Hill decided it was time to hang up his helmet and let another driver take his place on the team. That driver was a young talent by the name of Tony Brise, whom Hill had had his eye on for a while.

Tragically, though, a few months after announcing his retirement, Hill was dead, along with Brise and four other members of the team. They were returning from a test session at the Paul Ricard circuit in France, with Hill at the helm of his Piper Aztec light aircraft. He was struggling to land at Elstree airfield in thick fog and the plane crashed, killing all on board.

On that fateful night in November 1975, Britain lost a national institution. A man who was as at home appearing with Morecombe and Wise on television as he was behind the wheel of a racing car.

JAMES**HUNT**

Nationality: British

Born: 1947

Died: 1993

Seasons: 1973-1979

Teams: Hesketh, McLaren, Wolf

World Titles: 1 (1976)

Did you know?

The Hesketh race team has the unusual honour of being the only Formula One team ever to carry a grand piano in its cargo! Furthermore, the cars had no sponsorship, only a teddy bear logo.

ames Hunt came from a middle-class background and grew up in Berkshire, the on of a stockbroker. After a public school education, he was to follow a similar oute of respectability and become a doctor, but fate intervened. A friend took him o a motor race at Silverstone when he was 18 and he was instantly hooked.

The tumultuous teenager decided there and then he was going to be a Formula One Vorld Champion, and bought a wrecked Mini, which he spent the next two years race-reparing, much to his parents' disgust.

Hunt made a name for himself as a good, if rather accident-prone, driver and soon raduated to Formula Ford and Formula Three. His many accidents became legendary nd earned him the nickname of Hunt the Shunt. In one memorable incident, his ormula Ford car ended up in a lake and he may well have drowned if he'd been wearing harness, but he had been unable to afford one!

Perhaps part of the reason for his crashes was Hunt's nerves. He never conquered his re-race worries and was known to vomit and shake uncontrollably in the pit lane. This urned to adrenaline and testosterone on the track, though, which gave him a reputation s a bit of a madman.

For this reason, his career may have ended then if it hadn't been for the intervention of is friend, Lord Alexander Hesketh. Hesketh was extremely wealthy and liked to njoy life to the full, so he decided to start is own racing team, with Hunt as driver.

They started off in Formula Two and hree, with plenty of champagne and lamourous women to support them. Iowever, Hesketh argued that, if they were oing to lose money in motorsport, they night as well do it in Formula One.

The other teams treated Hesketh Racing s a joke at the start of the 1974 season, ut soon changed their minds when Hunt egan to put in some spectacular erformances and went on to beat Niki auda's Ferrari to win the 1975 Dutch

BELOW

James Hunt in action in his McLaren Ford during 1976.

Grand Prix. Sadly, at the end of the season, Lord Hesketh decided he could no longer afford to plough money into the team.

Luckily, though, McLaren needed a driver for 1976, and Hunt was the only available person with any experience. By the end of the season, Hunt was vying with Niki Lauda for the Championship and it came to a showdown at the last race in Japan. Lauda, though, decided it was too wet and retired from the race; he'd just recovered from a bad accident, and didn't want to take any risks. This left Hunt to take third place, winning the Championship on points. His boyhood ambition was fulfilled.

From then on, Hunt was never able to match this achievement and retired from racing in 1979, claiming that he'd never really enjoyed it!

By this time, he'd gained a reputation for being a wild character, enjoying drink, woman and partying. His combination of upper-class accent, quick temper and scruffy appearance, meant he was rarely out of the news, even after he'd retired.

Lacking direction, he started to commentate on Formula One for the BBC. Working alongside Murray

LEFT

Hunt storms to victory at the 1977 Race of Champions in the UK.

FAR LEFT

Hunt cooling off at the 1976 British Grand Prix at Brands Hatch.

BELOW

A relaxed James Hunt in front of the chequered flag in 1993.

/alker, the two became well known for their entertaining ut well-informed banter.

At the same time, Hunt's personal life began to settle own, and he married for a second time and had two hildren, to whom he was devoted. However, his wife left im for the actor Richard Burton. He then met Helen, a londe half his age, to whom he proposed to on 15th ıne 1993. She accepted but, tragically, just hours later, lunt had a massive heart attack and died. He was just 46 ears old.

On hearing of his death, Hunt's friend and rival, Niki auda, said: "For me, James was the most charismatic haracter who's ever been in Formula One."

NIKI **LAUDA**

Nationality: Austrian
Born: 1949
Seasons: 1971-1985
Teams: March, BRM, Ferrari, Brabham, McLaren
World Titles: 3 (1975, 1977, 1984)

Did you know?

When racing for Brabham, Niki Lauda drove a controversial car that used fan-assisted aerodynamics; a novel technology that was quickly banned from use in Formula One.

BELOW

Niki Lauda in action at the 1973 British Grand Prix, Silverstone.

Niki Lauda became a racing driver because he had the money to buy his way in. That said, he also proved himself an immense talent. Born in Vienna, his family were wealthy and well respected in Austria, and very much against Niki bringing the Lauda name into disrepute by becoming a racing driver. He spent his early teens driving around fields in an old Volkswagen Beetle convertible, and his first race was a hillclimb in a Cooper, before moving onto Formula Three.

His father refused to give Niki any financial help with his sport, so the determined youngster used his family name and connections to borrow large sums of money to fund his racing. By 1972 he had bought his way into the March Formula Two and Formula One teams, using money secured by his life insurance policy. The cars, however, were uncompetitive and Lauda was unable to prove himself as a driver.

With debts to repay, and no qualifications to do anything else, Lauda had no choice but to continue racing. He spent 1973 with BRM and was offered a paid-for place on the team for the following season, but was poached by Ferrari, who repaid his substantial debts and took him on as driver.

It was a good move all round, because Lauda won the first of 26 Formula One races in that first season with Ferrari. His cool and clinical approach to driving paid off and he finished fourth in the Championship, despite suffering a number of mechanical problems with his cars.

In 1975, Lauda and his Ferrari 312T dominated the season, with no less than five wins, and the Championship was his. He was on track to repeat his victory the following year when disaster struck. During the German Grand Prix at the Nürburgring, his car inexplicitly swerved and crashed, catching fire in the process. Four other drivers and a marshal came to Lauda's rescue, braving the inferno to drag him from the car.

Lauda suffered third-degree burns in the blaze, plus several broken bones and

scorched lungs. In fact, his injuries were so severe he was not expected to recover and a priest administered the last rites in hospital.

But, despite all the odds, the plucky Austrian made a miraculous recovery and, just six weeks later, he was at the Italian Grand Prix. With blood seeping from the bandages on his head, the determined driver finished in fourth place. However, the crash had shaken him to the extent that he pulled out of the Japanese Grand Prix later that year because of torrential rain, which he claimed was too dangerous to drive in. It was a decision that lost him the title to James Hunt.

However, in 1977, Lauda won the Championship back again, but then left Ferrari because he felt the team had not supported him after his crash the previous season.

From there, Lauda moved to Brabham where he finished fourth in the Championship in 1978. The following year, though, he struggled with an uncompetitive car and announced his retirement, saying he was "tired of driving around in circles".

Ready for a new challenge, he formed his own airline, Lauda Air, with him as one of the pilots. In order for this new company to grow, though, Lauda needed to raise some capital, so he returned to Formula One, after signing with McLaren for a reputed US$5 million. He joked that he was

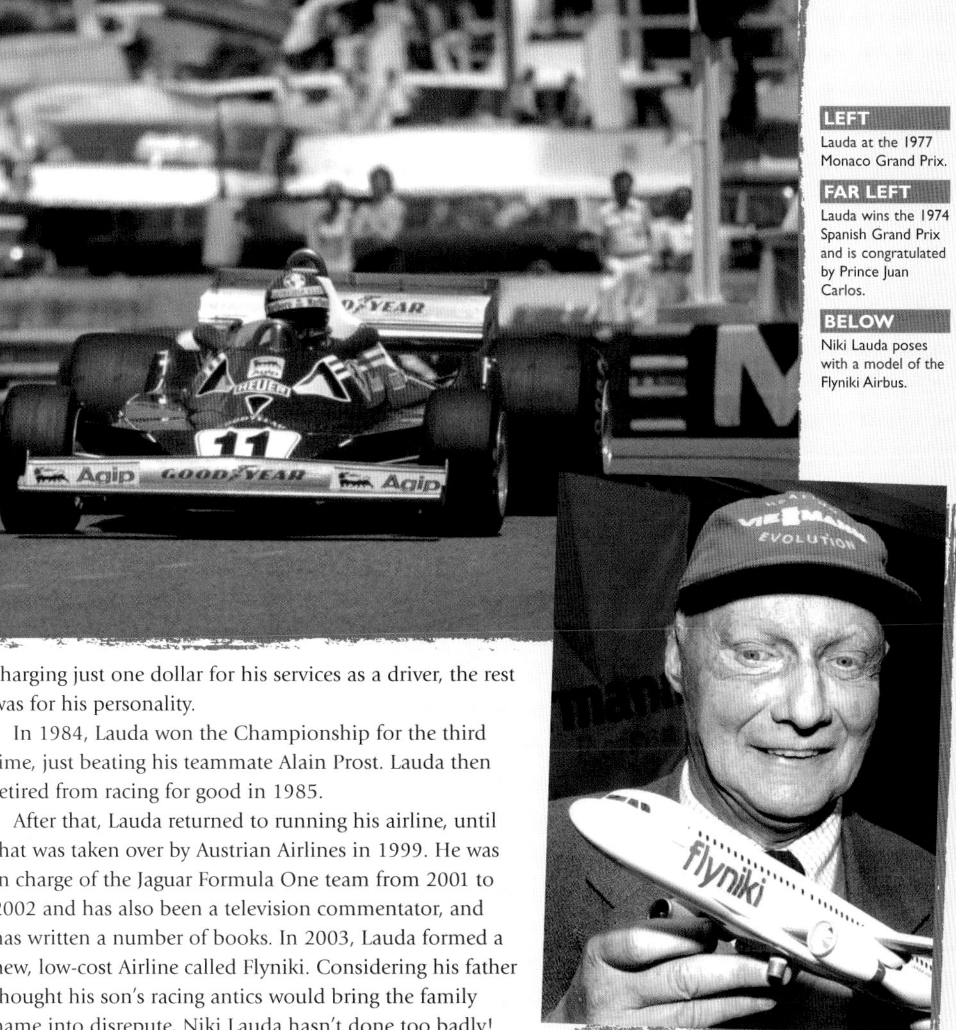

LEFT
Lauda at the 1977 Monaco Grand Prix.

FAR LEFT
Lauda wins the 1974 Spanish Grand Prix and is congratulated by Prince Juan Carlos.

BELOW
Niki Lauda poses with a model of the Flyniki Airbus.

charging just one dollar for his services as a driver, the rest was for his personality.

In 1984, Lauda won the Championship for the third time, just beating his teammate Alain Prost. Lauda then retired from racing for good in 1985.

After that, Lauda returned to running his airline, until that was taken over by Austrian Airlines in 1999. He was in charge of the Jaguar Formula One team from 2001 to 2002 and has also been a television commentator, and has written a number of books. In 2003, Lauda formed a new, low-cost Airline called Flyniki. Considering his father thought his son's racing antics would bring the family name into disrepute, Niki Lauda hasn't done too badly!

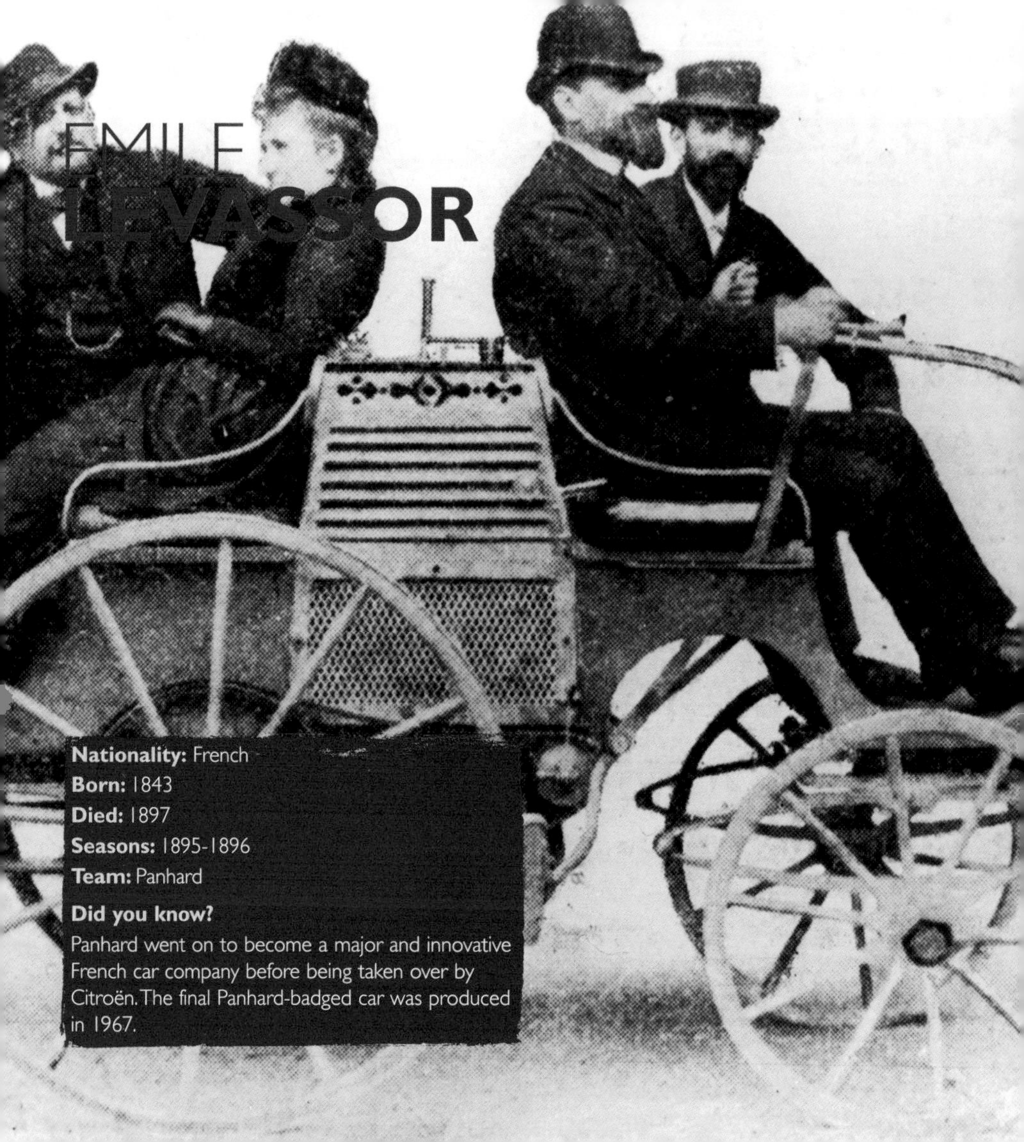

EMILE **LEVASSOR**

Nationality: French

Born: 1843

Died: 1897

Seasons: 1895-1896

Team: Panhard

Did you know?

Panhard went on to become a major and innovative French car company before being taken over by Citroën. The final Panhard-badged car was produced in 1967.

It all had to start somewhere; the glamour, excitement and money of Formula One. And it can be traced right back to the first-ever motor race. OK, it wasn't called a Grand Prix, but the 1895 Paris-Bordeaux-Paris race was the first proper motor race and had a large prize on offer. So, as such, it was the predecessor to today's Formula One. Organised by the Automobile Club de France, the 732-mile race attracted 46 entries. After 49 hours of almost non-stop driving, it was won by Emile Levassor, who had a handy six-hour lead on the next competitor. So Levassor became the first person to win a motorsport event. Ironically, he was later disqualified because it was argued that his car didn't have the four seats that the event's rules required. But it didn't matter – history had been made and motorsport was here to stay.

Levassor was the son of a farmer and was brought up in the countryside south of Paris. However, he gave up the rural life for a training in engineering and then went to work for an engineering company run by a former fellow student, Rene Panhard. By 1886 he was a partner in the company, now called Panhard & Levassor, and at this time, they were building engines that had been designed by Daimler.

When Daimler showcased one of its cars at the 1889 Exposition Universelle, a celebration of the 100th Anniversary of the French Revolution, demand for the engines grew and Levassor began to develop his own automobiles

After experimenting with a number of layouts, Levassor settled on the novel idea of mounting the engine in front of the driver, with a driveshaft to the rear wheels. With a total of four wheels, this configuration became known as the système Panhard. An advantage was a relatively low centre of gravity and the layout went on to became the standard for most cars. Something which alone would have assured Levassor a place in history.

It was in such a machine that Levassor drove to his historic victory, and there is no doubt that the car's front-engined

BELOW
Another Panhard Levassor car, this time on the 1902 Paris-Vienna race.

configuration contributed to his success. The racer was powered by a modest two-cylinder, 4bhp engine, and reached speeds of up to 10mph. It's interesting to note that another entrant in the race, André Michelin, had the radical idea of using pneumatic tyres on his Peugeot; a plan that was ridiculed by his competitors, who were using solid metal- or rubber-rimmed wheels.

The disqualification, due to the car having only two seats, deprived Levassor of the 31,000 Francs prize money, but history has been kinder to him – he is remembered for winning the race by a statue at the Porte Maillot in Paris, where the event finished.

The success led Panhard & Levassor to become a major player in the fledging motor industry, and Levassor worked at producing faster cars for competition use.

LEFT
After Levassor's death, Panhard Levassor cars continued to be developed and raced. This one is in the 1906 French Grand Prix.

FAR LEFT
An advertisement for a Daimler-designed Panhard & Levassor engine, similar to those fitted to the company's early cars.

Sadly, this was to lead to his undoing. In 1896, he was taking part in a Paris-Marseilles-Paris race and speeding downhill when a dog leapt out in front of him. Levassor swerved to avoid the animal and his car overturned, flinging him and his mechanic out. Levassor's chest impacted with the steering tiller and he suffered a broken rib and other internal injuries. Despite this, the pair righted the car and continued the race for a short time, until Levassor had to give up because of his painful injuries.

The accident weakened the engineer, but he refused to stop working. Levassor was in the process of designing a magnetic clutch when, in April 1897, he collapsed and died at his drawing board. He was 54 years old.

He may no longer be a household name, but Emile Levassor, by winning that race, became the first of many to celebrate success behind the wheel of a racing car.

NIGEL **MANSELL**

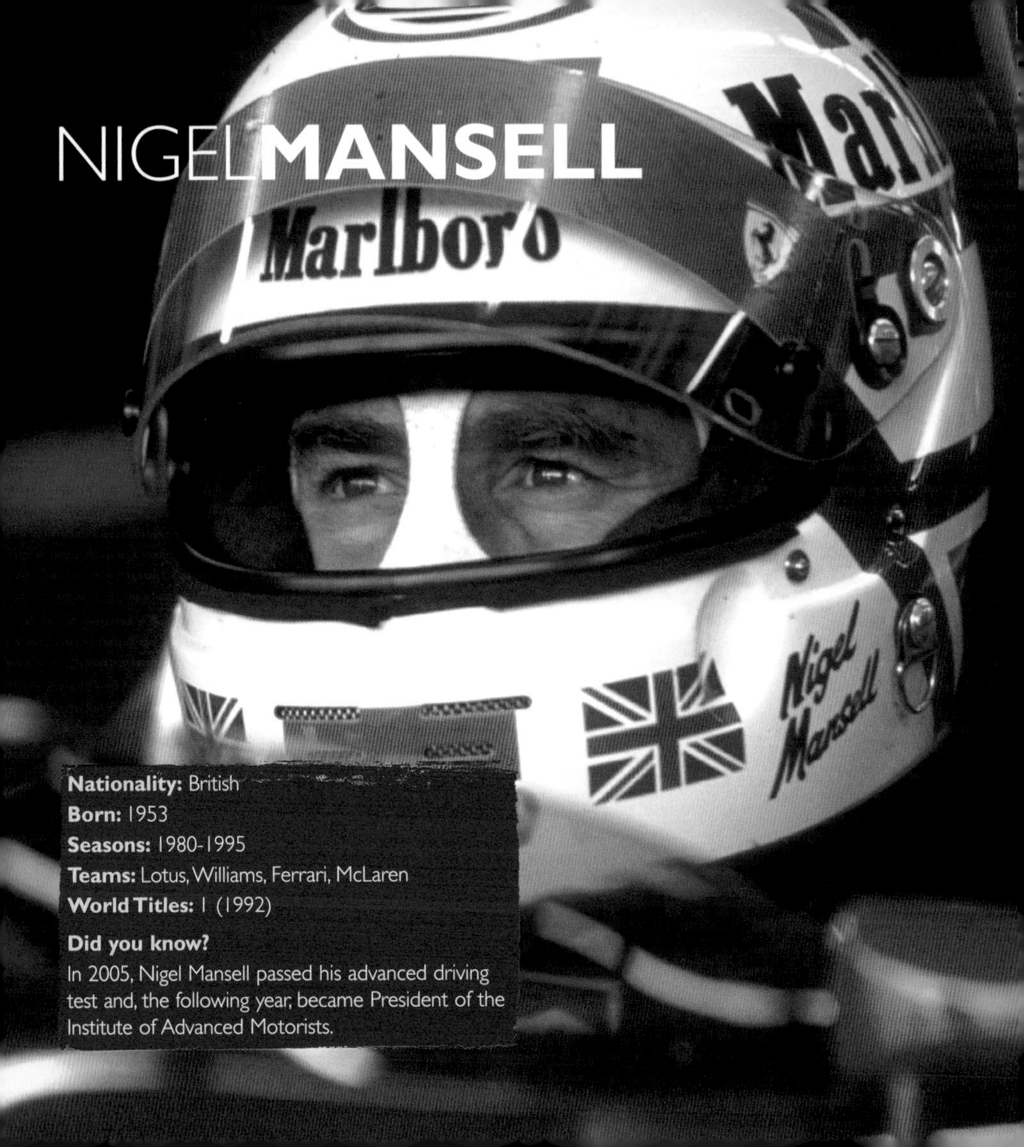

Nationality: British
Born: 1953
Seasons: 1980-1995
Teams: Lotus, Williams, Ferrari, McLaren
World Titles: 1 (1992)

Did you know?

In 2005, Nigel Mansell passed his advanced driving test and, the following year, became President of the Institute of Advanced Motorists.

Nigel Mansell, like many of the greatest drivers, started his career in karting. He gained his first licence at the tender age of 10, even though the minimum age was 11, and got straight on to the racing circuit. He won his first race when he was 14, using the simple philosophy that losing wasn't an option.

Mansell's father could see that his son had talent, but insisted that karting was fun, while motor racing was serious. With this in mind, the teenager invested £15 in a day's Formula Ford training. It paid off because, by 1977, he was Formula Ford Champion. That was despite breaking his neck in an accident during testing; an injury that doctor's said would cost him his racing career. Ignoring the advice to rest, Mansell sneaked out of hospital and raced on!

Determined to work his way up to Formula One, Mansell and his wife, Rosanne, sold their house and most of their belongings to fund a season in Formula Three for 1978. He did well and came second in the Championship, which secured him a place as a paid driver with Lotus the following year.

Once again, though, Mansell was hospitalised after a collision with another car. And, once again, he refused to give up. Dosed up with painkillers, he got out on track for a trial as a Formula One test driver with Lotus. Team boss, Colin Chapman was so impressed with Mansell's skills that he took him on as a Formula One driver from 1980.

Mansell spent the next four years with Lotus, but the cars didn't perform well enough for him to realise his full potential, with a third place finish the best he could manage. After Colin Chapman's sudden death in 1982, Mansell's relationship with Lotus became strained and he left the team to join Williams in 1985.

Now armed with better cars, Mansell immediately started to impress, gaining his first victory at Brands Hatch, followed by a second in Kyalami, South Africa. The following season, he performed even better,

BELOW
A dramatic close-up of Mansell's Williams at Brands Hatch in 1994.

with five wins and second place in the Drivers' Championship. In fact, he missed the Championship by just one point, and would have triumphed if it hadn't been for a burst tyre at Adelaide.

Mansell narrowly missed out on the Drivers' Championship again in 1987, when injuries sustained in an accident during qualifying at Suzuka caused him to miss the last race of the season, costing him valuable points.

After a disappointing 1988 season with Williams, Mansell moved to Ferrari in 1989, and was the last driver to be personally selected by Enzo Ferrari himself. Mansell was popular with Italian fans, who nicknamed him 'il leone' or 'the lion' because of his fearless driving style. He got off to a good start, too, with a win at the Brazilian Grand Prix. He won again at Hungary, after putting on an impressive show by working his way up from 12th place on the grid. Mansell finished fourth in the Championship that year.

Sadly, Mansell struggled with unreliable cars at Ferrari and was glad to return to Williams for the 1991 season. He finished second that year, but went on to win the Championship in 1992, after a record-breaking five race wins in a row at the start of the season.

The next year, Mansell fell out with Williams and raced in the CART Championship which he ended up winning, making him the only driver in history to hold both the Formula 1 World Championship and CART Championship at the same time.

LEFT
Mansell in his Honda-powered Williams at the Belgian Grand Prix, 1986.

FAR LEFT
Mansell celebrates winning the 1987 British Grand Prix.

BELOW
You can't keep a good man down! Mansell celebrates winning the 2005 Grand Prix Masters.

After the death of Ayrton Senna in 1994, Mansell returned o the Williams team for the end of the season and won the inal race in Adelaide.

However, he didn't stay with Williams, choosing instead o drive for McLaren in 1995. Unfortunately, he wasn't appy with the cars and announced his retirement from ormula One after just two races.

Since then, Mansell has made some brief returns to acing, including competing in the 1998 British Touring Car hampionship, and winning the Grand Prix Master Series ace in Kyalami in 2005.

Most recently, he's been helping to launch the careers of is sons, Greg and Leo in Formula BMW racing, and has sed his fame to help promote the series. Despite coming ite to racing, the young drivers appear to have inherited eir father's talent and look set to carry on the family name.

STIRLING**MOSS**

Nationality: British

Born: 1929

Seasons: 1951-1962

Teams: HWM, Connaught, Cooper, Maserati, Mercedes, Vanwall, Walker, BRP, Ferguson

Did you know?

Stirling Moss is reputed to have been stopped for speeding once, and the policeman asked him: "Who do you think you are, Stirling Moss?" The officer in question didn't expect the reply to be, "Yes"!

Stirling Moss is to motor-racing what David Bailey is to photography – a household name that people immediately associate with the sport. Even though he never quite won the World Championship, he was one of the greatest British drivers. Born in London in 1929, Moss came from a motorsport family because his father, Alfred Moss, was a regular at Brooklands, and also raced in the 1924 Indianapolis 500. His mother, meanwhile, was a keen trial and rally driver. It was no surprise then, that when he was nine, the young Stirling was given an old Austin Seven, which he tore around the local fields in.

Despite his parents' enthusiasm for cars, they didn't expect Moss to become a full-timer driver. Instead, they wanted him to take the sensible route and be a dentist, like his father. However, a poor academic record put paid to that plan and, at the age of 17, he reluctantly went to work in a hotel.

The teenager continued to take an interest in cars, though, and soon ordered an Aspen-engined racecar without telling his parents. His father was, not surprisingly, furious and cancelled the order when he found out. However, when he realised his son's disappointment, he let him use his BMW sports car for local speed trial events.

Before long, Moss had proved his worth as a driver and, with his parent's help, he bought a Cooper 500 racecar when he was just 18. He used this for hillclimbing and whatever other forms of racing he could enter. Before long, Moss was winning more than his fair share of races, with his supportive parents tagging along at weekend events.

Moss was soon noticed by team managers and, in 1950, he was asked to drive for the HWM Formula Two team. The following year, he was meant to be racing for Ferrari, but the team went back on their word and Moss vowed his revenge against the Italian team.

He first competed in Formula One in 1954, in a privately-owned Maserati 250F.

BELOW
Moss in action at the 1956 Grand Prix at Silverstone.

Moss created enough of an impression for Mercedes to sign him for the following season, where he was lucky enough to be teamed with Juan-Manuel Fangio, whom he beat to win the British Grand Prix. Moss wondered if Fangio let him win this race, but when he asked the Argentinean this, he was told: "No, you were just better than me that day."

After a brief stint with Maserati in 1956, Moss signed to Vanwall for 1957, arguing that he preferred to drive for a British team. This was a time of great success, with Moss winning no less than six Grands Prix in 1957 and 1958. In the latter year, he was very close to winning the Championship, but when his rival, Mike Hawthorn, was accused of rule-breaking in Portugal, Moss came to his defence, allowing Hawthorn to keep his points for that race. It was an admirable and typically sportsmanlike thing for Moss to do, but it did mean he lost the Championship to Hawthorn by just one point. It's also interesting to note that Moss won four Grands Prix that year, compared to just one for Hawthorn.

Perhaps one of the reasons such a great driver never quite won the Championship was because he often chose to drive British cars which, at the time, were not as competitive as some of their rivals. That

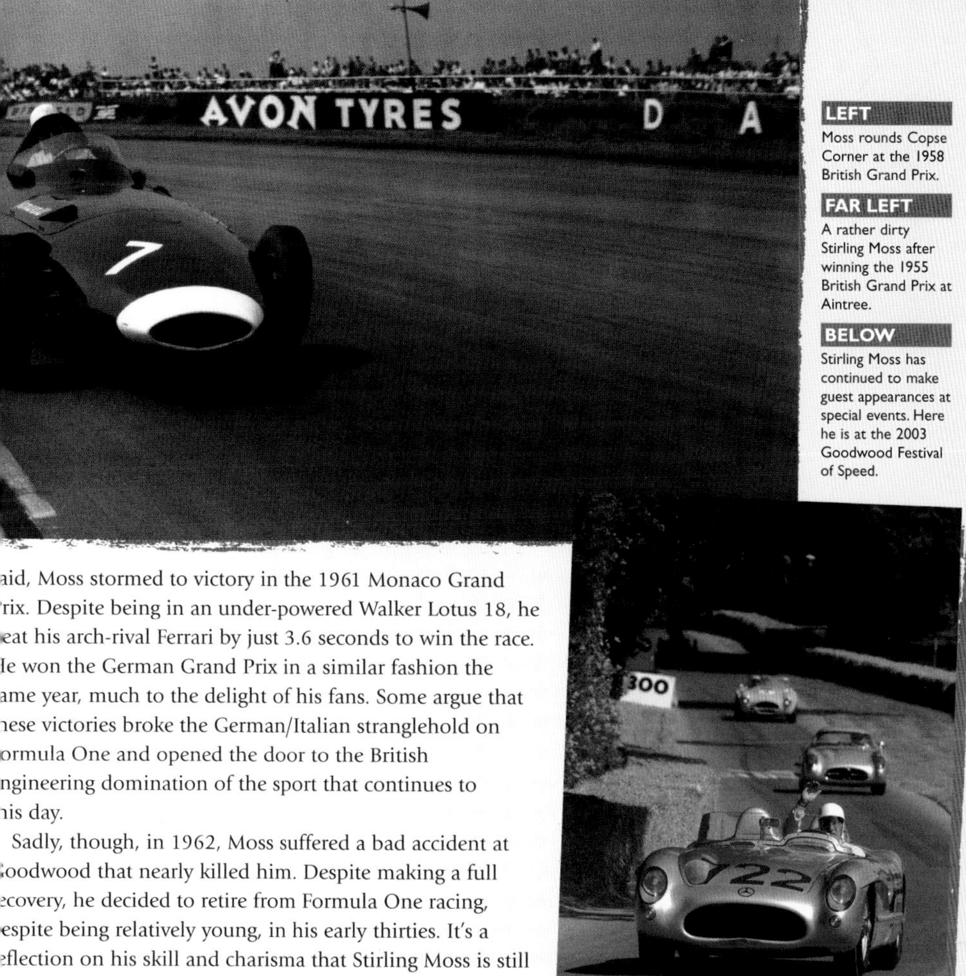

LEFT
Moss rounds Copse Corner at the 1958 British Grand Prix.

FAR LEFT
A rather dirty Stirling Moss after winning the 1955 British Grand Prix at Aintree.

BELOW
Stirling Moss has continued to make guest appearances at special events. Here he is at the 2003 Goodwood Festival of Speed.

aid, Moss stormed to victory in the 1961 Monaco Grand 'rix. Despite being in an under-powered Walker Lotus 18, he eat his arch-rival Ferrari by just 3.6 seconds to win the race. Ie won the German Grand Prix in a similar fashion the ame year, much to the delight of his fans. Some argue that ıese victories broke the German/Italian stranglehold on ormula One and opened the door to the British ngineering domination of the sport that continues to ıis day.

Sadly, though, in 1962, Moss suffered a bad accident at ;oodwood that nearly killed him. Despite making a full ecovery, he decided to retire from Formula One racing, espite being relatively young, in his early thirties. It's a eflection on his skill and charisma that Stirling Moss is still ne of the best-known names in motorsport over forty ears later.

TAZIO **NUVOLARI**

Nationality: Italian

Born: 1892

Died: 1953

Seasons: 1928-1946

Team: Alfa Romeo, Bugatti, Maserati, Auto Union

Did you know?

The poet Gabriele D'Annunzio presented Tazio Nuvolari with a little golden turtle engraved with the words "To the fastest man in the world, the slowest animal". Nuvolari considered this to be a good-luck charm and used it as his personal crest, embroidered on his racing clothes and printed on his stationery.

BELOW

Nuvolari driving an Auto Union to victory at the 1938 Grand Prix at Donington.

ne of the greatest drivers of the pre-war years (some would say of all time), Tazio ıvolari was the son of an Italian farmer but took little interest in his father's work, eferring the antics of his uncle, who was a champion cyclist and, later, otorcyclist. Indeed, it was his uncle, Giuseppe, who let the 12-year-old Tazio ride a otorbike for the first time.

Just a year later, the lively lad stole his father's car and drove it around after dark. His ssion for cars and bikes was irrepressible and, by the age of 23, he had a licence to race ɔtorbikes. However, the First World War intervened, and Nuvolari found himself in the ny driving lorries and ambulances during the hostilities.

After the war, Nuvolari finally got to take part in his first motorcycle race, in 1920, but d to retire from it. A year later saw him behind the wheel of a racing car for the first ne and he finished first in the reliability trial.

Nuvolari made quite a name for himself racing motorcycles but he wanted to progress o four-wheeled competition, so he started his own racing team. In conjunction with end and rival racer, Achille Varzi, he bought four Bugatti Grand Prix cars and drove one victory in the Tripoli Grand Prix.

From there, it was one success after another and Nuvolari's fame as an accomplished ver grew. By the start of the 1930s, he was driving for Alfa Romeo. Despite ing 37 years old and behind the wheel often inferior cars, he dominated and Prix racing, and won the Monaco, nch and Italian Grands Prix in 1932.

However, his most famous victory came 1935 at the German Grand Prix. The st country was confident of success with superior Auto Union and Mercedes nz cars, and Adolf Hitler himself was sent to watch. Imagine his surprise, n, when an Italian in an outdated car rmed through to finish first. It's said t Hitler was so outraged that he refused shake Nuvolari's hand after the race.

What's more, the Germans were so confident of a win, they didn't have the music to play the Italian national anthem!

Ironically, after another year racing with Alfa Romeo, Nuvolari moved to Auto Union for 1938, and proved himself more than capable of adapting to the powerful, rear-engined cars. He drove to victory at Donington and Monza that year. Then, in 1939, he won the last ever race that Auto Union would compete in, at Belgrade, before the Second World War put a stop to the company's activities.

After the war Nuvolari continued racing, despi suffering the tragic deaths of both his teenage so to illness. In 1946 he won three races for Masera and just one the following year.

By 1947, Nuvolari was 55 years old and not in good health. However, nothing would stop him from competing in that year's Mille Miglia. Behir the wheel of a Cisitalia 202, he struggled with fatigue, vomiting and bad weather to lead for mc of the race, finally finishing in second place.

LEFT

Nuvolari racing an Alfa Romeo during the 1930 Ulster Tourist Race, which he won.

FAR LEFT

Nuvolari is carried shoulder high as he celebrates his Ulster victory.

BELOW

Tazio Nuvolari at the wheel circa 1930. He was nicknamed 'Il Campionissimo' – The Great Little Man.

He attempted the Mille Miglia again the following year, is time in a Ferrari lent by none other than Enzo Ferrari mself, but victory eluded him once more.

Nuvolari's last race was the Palermo-Montepellegrino llclimb in 1950. Finishing first in class, it was also to be s last win. Ill-health overtook him, and he died at home 1953.

Ferdinand Porsche said that Nuvolari was "the greatest lot of the past, the present and the future." He could well ve been right.

NELSON PIQUET

Nationality: Brazilian
Born: 1952
Seasons: 1978-1991
Teams: Ensign, Brabham, Williams, Lotus, Benetton
World Titles: 3 (1981, 1983, 1987)

Did you know?

In January 2006, Nelson Piquet won the Brazilian 1000 miles event, driving an Aston Martin DB9R alongside his son. Exhausted at the end of the race, Piquet claimed he'd never race again!

The triple World Champion from Brazil was born Nelson Piquet Souto Maior and, as the son of a government minister, he had a privileged upbringing. Like his father, the youngster was a talented tennis player and was sent to sports school in San Francisco to develop this talent. However, while in the USA, Piquet became more interested in motor racing, something his father strongly disapproved of.

Determined to race, though, the strong-willed boy got involved in karting, using his mother's maiden name, but spelled 'Piket' at this time (you have to question the thinking here; surely his father would have seen through that one!). Before long, he'd established himself as a competent driver and went on to win the Brazilian Championship in his second year.

His father still wasn't impressed, though, and insisted that his son returned to the USA to study engineering at university. However, Piquet continued racing when he could and, by 1976, he was in a position to compete in – and ultimately win – the Brazilian SuperVee Championship.

Determined to go against his parent's wishes, Piquet moved to Europe in 1977 to race in Formula Three. He got off to a good start, finishing third in the Championship in his first year. He did even better in 1978, winning no less than 13 races in the British Formula Three Championship and walking away with the title.

Not surprisingly, this success gained him the attention of a number of Formula One teams and Piquet was quickly signed up by Brabham, to drive alongside Niki Lauda the following season. After a promising first season, in 1980 Piquet was promoted to team leader, following Lauda's supposed retirement, and gained his first Grand Prix win, at Long Beach. By the end of the season, he was within a point of winning the Championship, just behind Alan Jones. Piquet went on to have a storming season in 1981, winning the Drivers' Championship.

BELOW
A close-up of Piquet's Benetton-Ford at the 1990 German Grand Prix.

The next year was less successful, though, because Brabham was experimenting with a new turbocharged BMW engine. Piquet won in Canada but was otherwise frustrated by mechanical problems.

It proved to be time well spent in development, though, because the next season, Piquet made good use of the powerful new engine and went head to head with Alain Prost to take the Championship for a second time. Prost's Renault team claimed that the Brazilian was running on rocket fuel!

A couple of disappointing seasons followed with Brabham, and Piquet finally left the team in 1986 and signed up with Williams. Sadly, his first season was marred by disagreements with te who refused to play supporting role t argument that probably cost Piquet tl year. In 1987, though, he managed tc despite not winning as many races as to secure the Drivers' Championship

A move to the ailing Lotus team, in salary, in 1988 was to prove disastrous wins that year, and a similarly disappo

Now a shadow of his former self, F Benetton team in 1990 and managed

LEFT

A moody rear shot of Piquet's Lotus entering the tunnel at the 1989 Monaco Grand Prix.

FAR LEFT

Nelson Piquet at Brands Hatch in 1983, when he was driving for Brabham.

plus one the following season. However, it was not a good enough performance to persuade any team to offer him the sort of money he demanded for a place in 1992, so Piquet headed off to the USA to compete there. However, he was badly injured in practice for the Indianapolis 500, so he retired from racing and went back to his home country.

By now a very wealthy man, Piquet pursued a number of business interests in Brazil and continued to compete in sports car racing, but perhaps more for fun than serious intent.

However, his son, known as Nelson Piquet Junior, is making a name for himself in British Formula Three and, at the age of 19, became the youngest driver to win the Championship, in 2004. He's on track to be a future Formula One star and, unlike his father, this Nelson Piquet has the full support of his family!

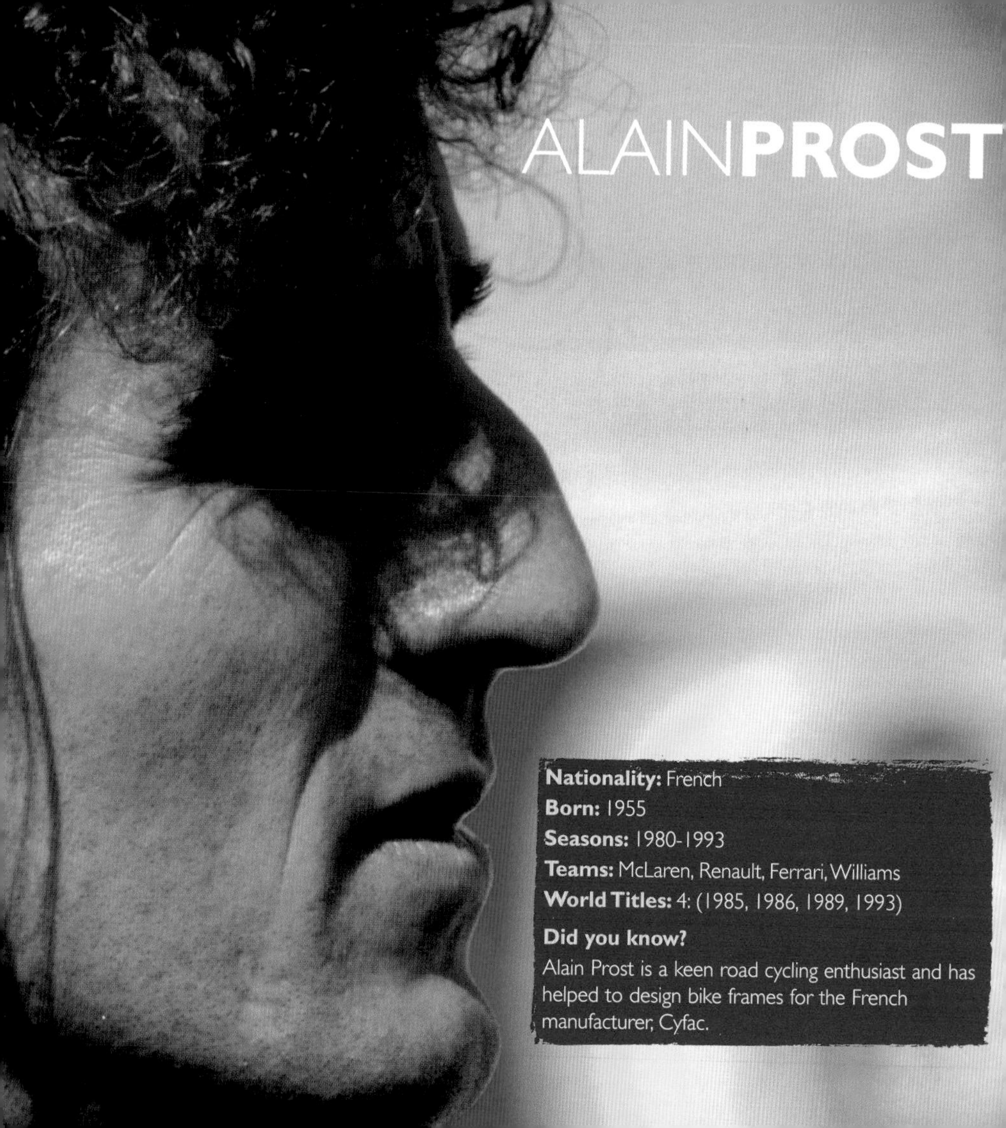

ALAIN **PROST**

Nationality: French

Born: 1955

Seasons: 1980-1993

Teams: McLaren, Renault, Ferrari, Williams

World Titles: 4: (1985, 1986, 1989, 1993)

Did you know?

Alain Prost is a keen road cycling enthusiast and has helped to design bike frames for the French manufacturer, Cyfac.

With no less than four World Championship titles to his name and winner of an incredible 51 Grands Prix, statistically Alain Prost is second only to Michael Schumacher as the most successful Formula One driver ever. And yet, as a boy, Prost wanted to be a professional footballer and probably would have done very well in that sport. Thankfully for the world of motorsport, though, he got involved in karting as a teenager and soon realised that this was more fun than kicking a football. By the age of 18, he had won the European Junior Karting Championship and went on to compete in other karting events around Europe.

In 1975, Prost entered the Volant Elf competition and won a drive in the Formula Renault Championship the following year. To everyone's astonishment, this newcomer dominated the Championship and walked away with the title.

Such an astonishing performance persuaded Renault to promote Prost to Formula Three for 1978. After struggling with a substandard car in his first season, the Frenchman went on to win the both the French and European Formula Three Championships in 1979. These were achievements that did not go unnoticed in the world of Formula One, and the promising new talent was signed by the McLaren team for the 1980 season.

Sadly, Prost's debut in Formula One was marred by mechanical failures, one of which led to a minor crash that caused him to break a wrist. Despite this, the newcomer out-drove teammate, John Watson, to finish the Championship in a respectable sixth place. However, Prost was not happy with McLaren and broke his contract to move to Renault the following year.

Excitedly for his fellow countrymen, Prost won his first Formula One race on home turf at the French Grand Prix in 1981. He did well with Renault, getting better and better and, finally, coming second in the World Championship in 1983, behind Nelson Piquet. However, there was constant pressure on him to be

BELOW

Alain Prost on a lap of honour at the Portuguese Grand Prix, after winning the World Championship in 1993.

the first French World Champion driving a French car, so Prost returned to McLaren for 1984.

The team had, by this time, been taken over by Ron Dennis and was producing much better cars than before. So good, in fact, that Prost was once again runner-up at the end of 1985, second only to teammate Niki Lauda. And in 1985 he won his first Championship title; a success he repeated the following year, making him the first driver to win twice in a row since Jack Brabham in 1959 and 1960.

Prost himself recommended that McLaren sign Ayrton Senna as his teammate for 1988, and the pair dominated the series, with Prost coming second place to Senna in the Championship. However, the following year led to confrontation between the two drivers, with Prost accusing Senna of taking unnecessary risks on track, saying; "Ayrton thinks he can't kill himself because he believes in God and I think that is very dangerous for other drivers."

The rivalry came to a head at the Japanese Grand Prix, when Prost knew that, if neither driver finished, he would win the Championship on points. The two McLarens collided and Prost retired from the race, but Senna continued, after being given an illegal push-start by the marshals, for which he was disqualified, ensuring that Prost won the Championship.

In 1990, the tables were turned, though, and Senna deliberately drove into Prost, who was now driving for Ferrari, to ensure that Senna would clinch the title. Prost stayed with

LEFT

A jubilant Alain Prost winning the Australian Grand Prix in 1988.

FAR LEFT

Prost celebrates winning the Monaco Grand Prix, 1988.

BELOW

Prost at Silverstone in 2000, when he was running his own team.

Ferrari for 1991 but he was dismissed before the end of the season for being publicly critical of the team.

There was no time to sign to another outfit for 1992, but Prost found himself driving for Williams in 1993. With seven wins that year, he easily took the Drivers' Championship for a fourth time. Despite his success, though, Williams decided to drop the Frenchman in favour of Ayrton Senna, and so Prost retired from Formula One.

That was not to be the end of his involvement in the sport, though. Prost became a commentator on Formula One for French television and worked as a consultant for Renault and then McLaren. In 1997 he bought the Ligier team and renamed it Prost Grand Prix. Sadly, the team was not a great success and finally went bankrupt in 2002. Thankfully, Alain Prost is remembered for what he was really good at – winning in Formula One.

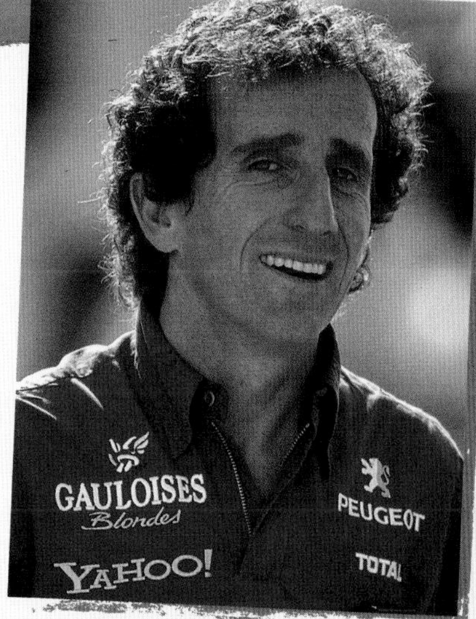

BERND**ROSEMEYER**

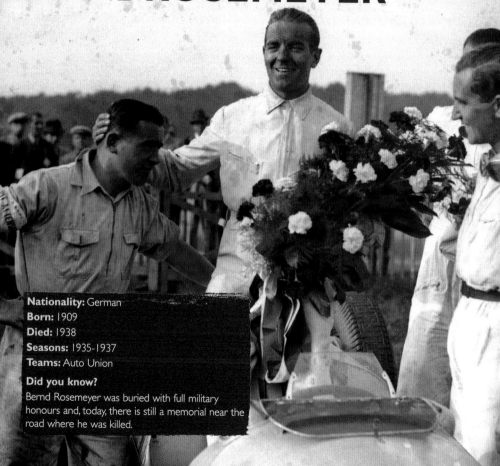

Nationality: German

Born: 1909

Died: 1938

Seasons: 1935-1937

Teams: Auto Union

Did you know?

Bernd Rosemeyer was buried with full military honours and, today, there is still a memorial near the road where he was killed.

BELOW

Rosemeyer (number 6) lapping two ERAs in his V16 Auto Union at Donington in 1937.

'or two brief years, Bernd Rosemeyer was the fastest Grand Prix driver in the vorld, driving the almighty mid-engined Auto Union cars in the 1935s. Sadly, ragedy was to strike before this great talent was fully realised. Born in Germany's .ower Saxony, the young Rosemeyer grew up around motorcycles and cars, working ıt his father's garage business. As a teenager, he started racing motorcycles and ;ained a reputation for being a fast rider with a fun personality. He got involved vith the DKW factory, which had recently joined forces with three other nanufacturers to form the Auto Union group.

Auto Union was developing an exciting new Grand Prix car, with the help of Ferdinand 'orsche. It was unlike any other racecar, with a mid-mounted V16 engine to give better-alanced handling. In those days, cars had the engine mounted at the front, and it was to e another 30 years before the mid-engined concept was fully adopted in motorsport. Vith supercharged power and fully independent suspension, the Auto Unions really were head of their time.

Unfortunately, though, they were also very tricky to drive, mainly because the ıdependent suspension wasn't fully developed. Rosemeyer, however, knew nothing of ıis, only that the cars sounded radical and exciting, and he was determined to drive one. fter much pestering, the team manager, Willy Walb, agreed to let Rosemeyer y the car at the notorious Nürburgring.

Rosemeyer turned up for his drive 'earing a suit. When Walb asked him why e'd dressed up, Rosemeyer replied that it 'as a special occasion – his first drive in a ıcing car. Walb wasn't sure what to make f the young man, but after he'd seen him n the track, he was impressed. The Auto nion had ten times the horsepower of osemeyer's motorcycles, but Rosemeyer on got the hang of the beast. Before ng, he was matching the times of the am's more experienced drivers, so Walb ecided to take him on as a reserve.

Ironically, it was Rosemeyer's lack of experience in driving racing cars that gave him an advantage – he just assumed that the Auto Union's characteristics were normal.

Rosemeyer's first race was at the Avus Grand Prix, near Berlin, in 1935. Despite qualifying third, he was unable to finish the race because of engine problems. The next race was at the Nürburgring, which Rosemeyer knew well from his motorcycle days, and the newcomer went head to head with Rudolf Caracciola to finish in second place; he may well have won if it hadn't been for a misfiring engine. Team boss, Walb, was impressed enough to promote Rosemeyer from reserve to full-time driver.

At his next race, at Percara in Italy, Rosemeyer would once again challenge one of the greats; this time Tazio Nuvolari. Rosemeyer attempted to pass the Italian, but skidded off the track, bursting two tyres. Not to be outdone, he returned to the pits, had the tyres replaced, and rejoined the race, finally finishing in second place.

Rosemeyer had his first win at his next race, the Brno Masaryk Grand Prix in Czechoslovakia, where he beat Nuvolari by a full six minutes. The newcomer had thrown down the gauntlet to the establishment.

In 1936, Rosemeyer took the Grand Prix world by storm, starting with an astonishing win at the Nürburgring. In thick

LEFT
Rosemeyer testing an Auto Union on the Avus track in Berlin in 1937.

FAR LEFT
Bernd Rosemeyer at the Nürburgring in 1937. Although not a Nazi supporter, he had to be seen to be complying.

ɔg, he sped to victory, in near-impossible conditions. He also won the German, Pescara, wiss and Italian Grands Prix, thus securing the European Championship.

The following year saw Rosemeyer head to the USA, where he won the Vanderbilt Cup. Ie also did well in Europe, but failed to retain the Championship. His performances vith the mighty Auto Union were, though, enough for Mercedes to issue a challenge – hey wanted to reclaim the world speed record from Auto Union.

Rosemeyer agreed to meet on the Frankfurt-Darmstadt Autobahn on 28th January 938, where Rudolf Caracciola would be driving the Mercedes. Caracciola did his run nd set a new record of 268mph in the early morning. Rosemeyer was up next, but ;aracciola tried to talk him out of it because the wind was building off. Rosemeyer hrugged it off, saying he was lucky, and off he went. The streamlined Auto Union eached a speed of over 270mph when a crosswind flung it off the road, causing it to ɔmersault. Rosemeyer was thrown from the car and died at the roadside.

Bernd Rosemeyer's career was all too short, but he will always be remembered as one f the only people who could truly master the Auto Union racecars.

Nationality: German

Born: 1969

Seasons: 1991-

Teams: Jordan, Benetton, Ferrari

World Titles: 7 (1994, 1995, 2000, 2001, 2002, 2003, 2004)

Did you know?

Michael Schumacher is often ribbed for his taste in music, which is very much easy-listening. He's a fan of Celine Dion and Phil Collins, to name but two.

BELOW

A close-up of Schumacher's Ferrari at the practice session for the Grand Prix of Europe, 2006.

Statistically, Michael Schumacher is the most successful Formula One driver of all time. He's also the highest paid – with a reputed income of $80-million a year – and probably the most famous, too. As of 2006, Schumacher had won the Drivers' Championship no less than seven times and had come first in an amazing 84 races, and second in 40 races. He's also the only German to win a Formula One Championship.

That's not bad for someone who started racing a homemade kart at the age of five. His father, Rolf, built the machine and just happened to be manager of the kart track at Kerpen, the family's hometown.

The youngster soon proved himself handy behind the wheel and, at the age of 12, he began racing karts competitively. Throughout his teens, Schumacher won numerous kart Championships in Germany and Europe.

In 1988, at the age of 19, Schumacher raced in Formula Ford, moving to German Formula 3 for the following two years, and winning the Championship in 1990.

Schumacher drove for Jordan in the 1991 Belgian Grand Prix as a one-off, because he'd assured team boss, Eddie Jordan, that he knew the Spa circuit well. If the truth be known, though, the young German had only ever been round the track once – on a bicycle! Still, on this, his first Formula One race, Schumacher qualified seventh. Sadly, he had to retire from the race, but his performance was good enough to persuade Benetton to sign him for the rest of the season.

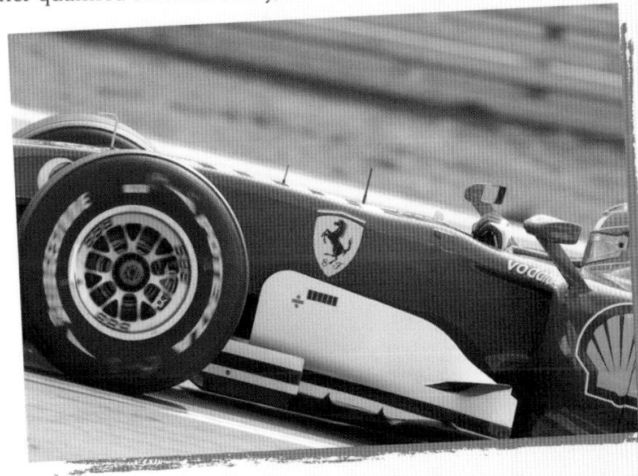

In 1992, Schumacher stayed with Benetton and won his first Formula One race at Spa – perhaps that trip round on a bike had been beneficial! He went on to finish his first full season in third place.

Schumacher stayed with Benetton and stormed to victory in 1994, by winning six of the first seven races of the season. This led to allegations of cheating by other teams, who maintained that the team was

using illegal electronic aids, such as traction control and adaptive suspension.

It was to prove to be a controversial season, with Schumacher sparring with Damon Hill in the last race at Adelaide, with allegations that he deliberated forced the Englishman to retire. Whatever happened, the fact remained that Schumacher won the Drivers' Championship by just one point. He repeated the success the next year, this time with a cool 30-point lead, which helped clinch the Constructors' Championship for Benetton.

Schumacher turned his back on the winning combination of driver and team in 1996 and moved to Ferrari, an ailing team that had not won a title since 1979. The car's might have not been up to scratch, but that didn't stop the German from finishing the season in third place.

The 1997 season brought more controversy for Schumacher, with him being disqualified from the World Championship after a collision with Jacques Villeneuve. Schumacher would have taken second place if it hadn't been for the decision by the FIA to punish him for the incident.

While this was happening, the Ferrari team was improving its cars, thanks in part to the efforts of the design team which Schumacher had coaxed from Benetton. Indeed, the team won the Constructors' title in 1999, but Schumacher had to wait another year before he would win the Drivers' Championship with Ferrari.

From then on, it was only good news for the German, with him winning the Championship again for the following four years in a row. His win in 2003 was his sixth, which beat the record previous held by Juan Manuel Fangio, and the next year he won

LEFT

Schumacher wins the San Marino Grand Prix, at Imola in 2006.

FAR LEFT

Schumacher's Ferrari on a wet Silverstone track in 2000.

BELOW

Michael Schumacher celebrating after winning the 2004 Malaysian Grand Prix.

3 races, thus breaking his own record of 11. There was no .olding the man back!

However, it was not to last. Schumacher failed to win in 005, dogged in part by new regulations that insisted that /res had to last for a whole race – a rule which some :eptics claimed was brought in purely to end Schumacher's nd Ferrari's domination of Formula One! Even so, he still nished in a respectable third place at the end of the season.

At the start of the 2006 season in Bahrain, Schumacher .atched Ayrton Senna's record by taking his 65th pole osition. Impressive as this may be, it's worth noting that it ook the German 233 races to match a record that Senna set 1 just 162 races.

Aged 37 in 2006, Schumacher is one of the oldest rivers in Formula One, yet is showing no signs of retiring nd, if he continues to excel, could well be World hampion once again.

HENRY**SEGRAVE**

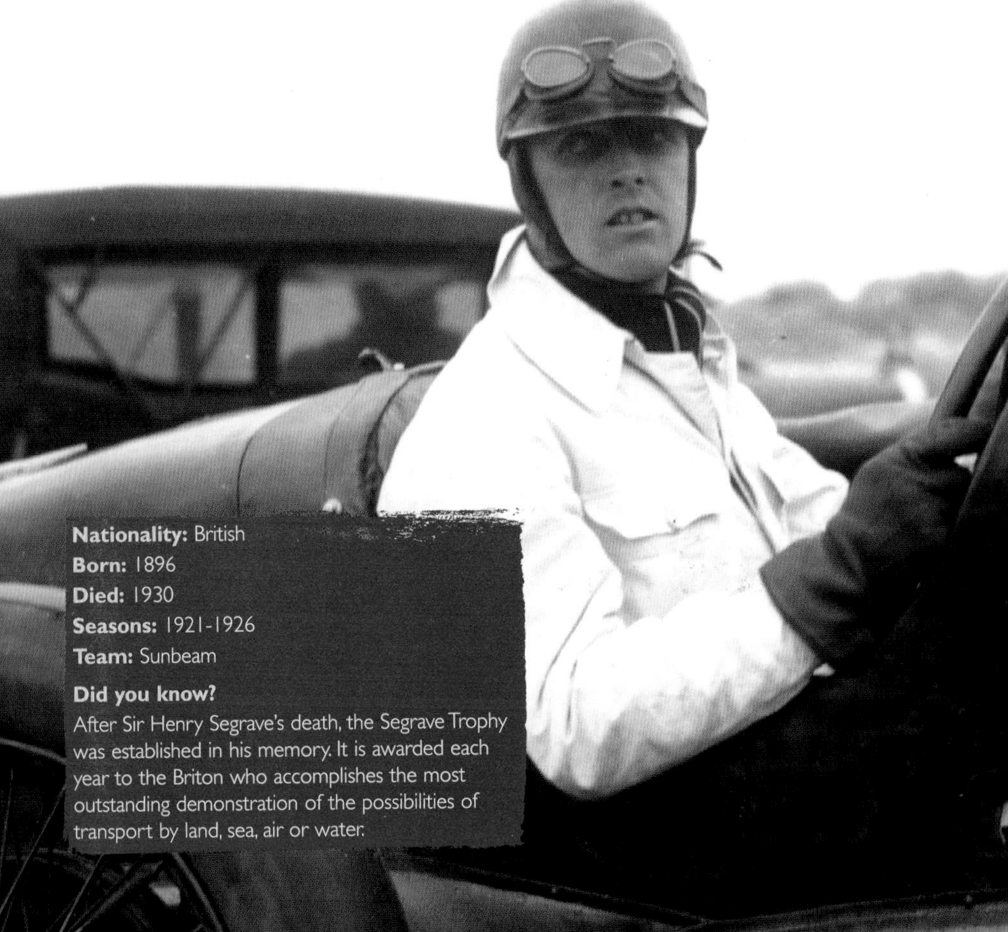

Nationality: British
Born: 1896
Died: 1930
Seasons: 1921-1926
Team: Sunbeam

Did you know?
After Sir Henry Segrave's death, the Segrave Trophy was established in his memory. It is awarded each year to the Briton who accomplishes the most outstanding demonstration of the possibilities of transport by land, sea, air or water.

Today, Sir Henry Segrave is better remembered for his record-breaking accomplishments. However, he also played a key role in the history of Grand Prix racing – by being the first ever British driver to win a Grand Prix. This daring driver was born in the USA, of an American mother and an Irish father. He was raised in Ireland and was educated at Eton College in England. He fought in the First World War and claimed then that he would one day drive a car at over 200mph, but his comrades laughed at him, claiming that the stresses of war had got to him.

After the war, Segrave watched a motor race in the USA and was hooked. He returned to England and started racing at Brooklands, eventually getting a place on the Sunbeam works team in 1921.

It was in 1923 that he had his historical win, which was in a Sunbeam at the French Grand Prix. The following year he won again, this time at the Spanish Grand Prix. After a final win in France in 1926 he gave up racing to concentrate on record-breaking attempts, and to achieve his dream of reaching 200mph in a car.

Working for Sunbeam, he was closely involved in the development of his record-breaking cars, and Segrave set his first land-speed record in 1926, when he reached a speed of 174.22mph in his 4-litre Sunbeam Ladybird, at Southport Sands in Lancashire.

The following year, Segrave's dream came true, when he became the first man to drive at over 200mph. His Mystery Sunbeam, with its 1000bhp engine, reached an amazing 203.79mph at Daytona.

In 1929, Segrave went on to beat his own record, this time in the now-famous Irving Napier Golden Arrow. Again at Daytona, he hit a top speed of 231.36mph. Amazingly, the car had just 18.74 miles on the clock after the record had been set, and has never been driven since. Soon after this, an American, Lee Bible, died in an attempt to break the record; a tragedy that led Segrave to turn his back on land-speed

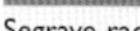
BELOW

Segrave racing a Sunbeam at the 1924 French Grand Prix.

records. Segrave was, however, knighted for his achievements.

However, he didn't turn his back on record-breaking. Far from it; but, instead of land, he moved to water. His first boat, Miss England I, was powered by the 900bhp engine from one of his cars. Although flawed in many ways, this craft taught Segrave much about speedboats, and he later produced a second, Miss England II. This was powered by a pair of incredible 2000bhp supercharged Rolls Royce engines, powering a tiny two-blade propeller at 12,000rpm.

The plan was to attempt to break the world record of 92.84mph, held by an American. On Friday 13th June, 1930, the 38-foot boat was launched at Lake Windermere in the Lake District. Segrave jokingly pointed out the unlucky date to his engineer and then they were off.

The stunning craft reached a speed of 101.11mph and then, on the next run, Segrave

tried even harder. For reasons that have never been explained, the boat shot out of the water and its crew was flung from the cockpit.

Segrave was pulled, unconscious, from the water and rushed to hospital. There, he regained consciousness for long enough for his wife to tell him that he had broken the record. He then died, aged just 34.

Perhaps his exciting record-breaking attempts have eclipsed his Grand Prix career, but Henry Segrave's success for Britain in the French Grand Prix of 1923 shouldn't be forgotten.

ABOVE
Segrave's 1000bhp Sunbeam record-breaker in 1927.

FAR LEFT
Segrave in civilian garb, looking an unlikely hero!

ARYTON**SENNA**

Nationality: Brazilian

Born: 1960

Died: 1994

Seasons: 1984-1994

Teams: Toleman, Lotus, McLaren, Williams

World Titles: 3 (1988, 1990, 1991)

Did you know?

Ayrton Senna donated large sums of money to children's charities, a fact he kept secret during his lifetime. After his death, his family formed the Ayrton Senna Foundation to help needy young people in Brazil and around the world.

BELOW
Senna's Lotus at the 1986 Hungarian Grand Prix.

For many, Ayrton Senna was the greatest racing driver of all time. After his tragic death in 1994, he became a sporting legend, never to be forgotten. It all began in Sao Paulo, where the young Senna grew up. Encouraged by his father, Senna began karting at the age of four but local regulations meant he was unable to compete until his was 13. His first races took place on made-up courses over streets and car parks, and the lad had an immediate advantage on the straights because he was younger and lighter than many of his competitors, although he then lacked the skills necessary for cornering.

Before long, though, Senna was competing seriously and in 1977, at the age of 17, he won the South American Kart Championship; a feat he went on to repeat the following year. He then travelled to Le Mans and came sixth in the World Championships.

By 1981, Senna was in England competing in Formula Ford 1600, and won the series in his first year. The following year he moved to Formula Ford 2000 and won both the British and European Championships.

In 1983, Senna won the Formula Three Championship and immediately got the attention of Formula One teams. After some negotiations, he was signed by the small British Toleman team (which later became Benetton and then Renault). He impressed in his first season, with an incredible performance at the very wet Monaco Grand Prix, where he worked his way up from 13th place to challenge leader, Alain Prost. However, the race was cancelled because of the weather before Senna could attempt to take the lead. He finished a respectable ninth in his first season, tying with Nigel Mansell.

For 1985, Senna moved to Lotus, despite still being contracted to Toleman, and had his first Grand Prix victory at Portugal where, again, he showed off his wet-weather ability. He finished the season in fourth place, as he did the following year. He did slightly better with Lotus in 1987, coming third in the Championship.

Senna moved to McLaren for the 1988 season, where he formed a formidable partnership with Alain Prost. Both superb drivers, they were often sparring with each other for victory. Indeed, that year the pair won 15 out of 16 races between them for McLaren, with Senna having the edge and winning his first World Championship.

The following year, the rivalry increased, with Prost taking the Championship after blocking Senna from overtaking at Suzuka. However, in 1990 the Brazilian got his own back by bumping Prost's car at the same circuit, causing both drivers to to retire, which clinched the Championship for Senna on points.

Part of Senna's success lay in his skill in qualifying, and he gained pole position in no less than 65 of the 161 races he entered, a record that stood until beaten by Michael Schumacher in 2006.

It's a record that Senna would surely have beaten if fate hadn't tragically intervened. In 1994 he was racing for Williams-Renault and the San Marino Grand Prix was already turning into a nightmare, with Senna's teammate, Rubens Barrichello in hospital after an accident on the Friday. Then, on the Saturday, Austrian Roland Ratzenberger was killed in practice, causing Senna to meet with other drivers to discuss safety issues in Formula one.

Senna almost retired there and then, but chose to continue and race at San Marino on the Sunday. He'd stuffed an Austrian flag into his cockpit, which he was going to raise in memory of Ratzenberger during his lap of honour – an act that would have been typical of Senna's compassionate nature.

LEFT

Senna in action at the 1990 Australian Grand Prix.

FAR LEFT

A young Senna at Brands Hatch in 1985, while driving for Lotus.

BELOW

Ayrton Senna adjusts his mirror before the start of the 1994 San Marino Grand Prix. He was killed in the seventh lap of the race.

However, it was not to be. During the race, Senna's ır left the track at a speed of 193mph, and hit an ıprotected concrete wall. He was killed instantly.

Senna's death, at the age of just 34, shocked the orld, and over a million people lined the streets of ıo Paulo for his memorial service. It also led to uch speculation on the cause of the accident, ith a lengthy inquiry clearing the Williams team blame.

It was a tragic and premature end to a great career, ıt Ayrton Senna's name lives on in the form of his ephew, Bruno Senna. Ayrton himself once said, "If u think I'm good, wait until you see my nephew, uno." And the youngster is already making a me for himself in Formula Three, wearing the me yellow and green helmet as his uncle.

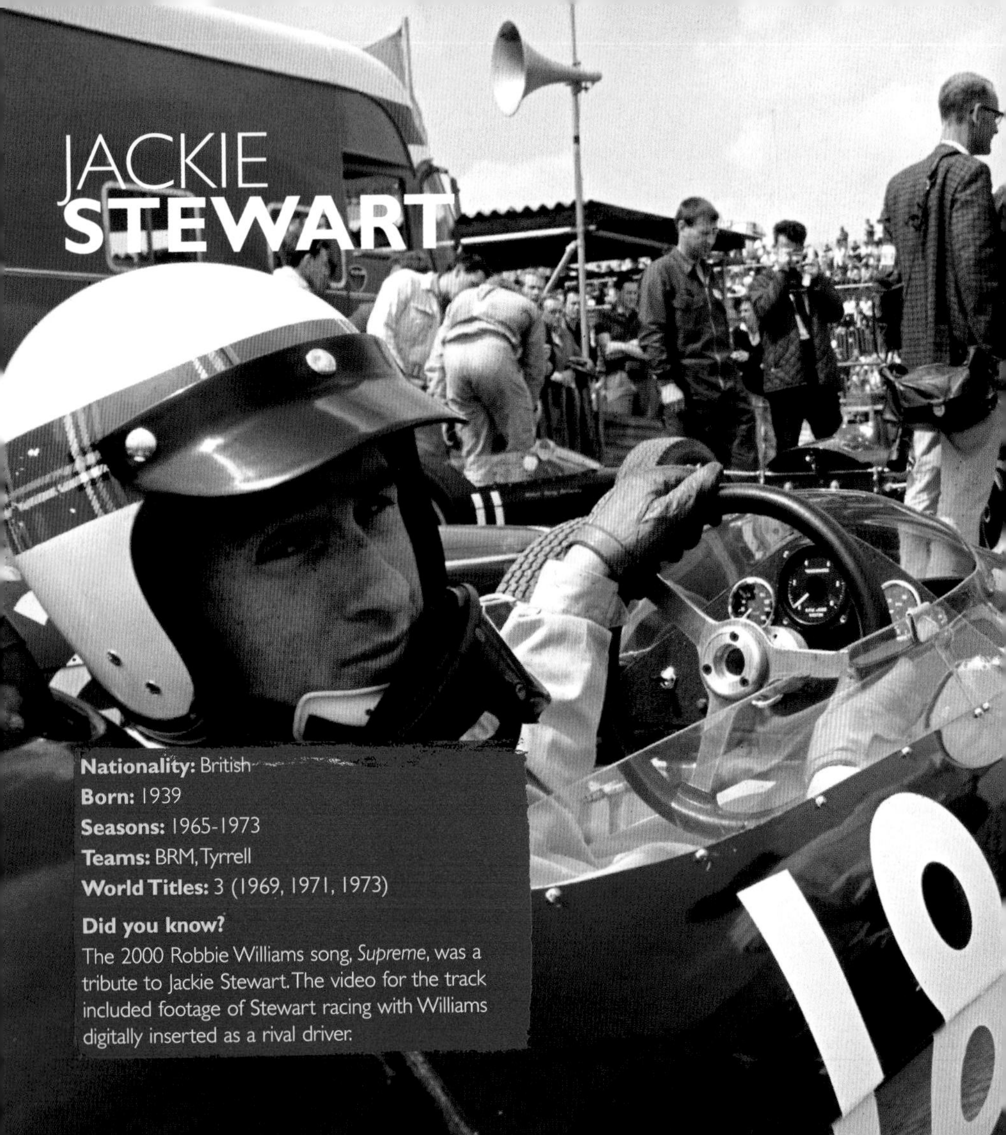

JACKIE STEWART

Nationality: British
Born: 1939
Seasons: 1965-1973
Teams: BRM, Tyrrell
World Titles: 3 (1969, 1971, 1973)

Did you know?

The 2000 Robbie Williams song, *Supreme*, was a tribute to Jackie Stewart. The video for the track included footage of Stewart racing with Williams digitally inserted as a rival driver.

ackie Stewart was born in 1939 and almost missed out on being a racing driver, ecause of the misfortune of his elder brother, Jimmy. Their father raced notorcycles and then ran a Jaguar dealership in Milton, Scotland, so speed was in he boys' blood.

Brother Jimmy was already making a name for himself in Grand Prix racing when the oung Jackie started work as an apprentice mechanic at his father's garage. However, after immy was injured in a crash at Le Mans, their parents decided that motor racing was erhaps not a suitable sport for their sons. Jackie, therefore, took up target shooting and lmost made it to the 1960s Olympics. Perhaps if he had done so, the world of Formula)ne would have missed out on one its most colourful characters.

As it turned out, one of his father's customers offered Stewart a try in some racecars at)ulton Park in 1963. He impressed everyone with his abilities and Ken Tyrrell asked him) test for the Cooper Formula Cooper team. Driving alongside Formula One driver, ruce McLaren, Stewart consistently put in the best times and Tyrrell wasted no time in ffering the young Scot a place on his Formula Three team.

Stewart won his first race for Tyrrell the following year, at Snetterton, but he was keen) move on to Formula One, something which Tyrrell was not involved in at the time. So iat meant a move to BRM, where he was signed for £4000, driving alongside raham Hill in the 1965 season. Stewart ɔt off to a good start, picking up a hampionship point in his first race, in ɔuth Africa. By the end of the season, e'd won at Monza and was honoured ith the Rookie of the Year award.

In 1966, an incident started Stewart off ı a lifelong campaign to improve safety Formula One. At the start of the Belgian rand Prix at Spa, he crashed his BRM and und himself stuck in the cockpit with el leaking all around him. The marshals ıd no tools to help him escape, and it was t to team-mate Graham Hill to rescue

Jackie Stewart driving for Tyrrell, on the way to winning the Dutch Grand Prix at Zandvoort in 1968.

him. Suffering from a broken collar bone, Stewart was then shocked at how long it took to get to hospital in a decrepit ambulance.

Stewart put forward the idea, which was adopted, that all racecars should have a removable steering wheel and a main battery isolator switch; sensible safety features that are still used today. He also made sure he had his own doctor on-hand at any subsequent race he competed in, while BRM supplied a medical truck for the benefit of all involved. Today, such onsite medical facilities are essential at any motorsport event.

As time went on, Stewart pushed for more safety equipment. Things such as full-face helmets, harnesses, safety barriers and run-off areas are commonplace today, but in the 1960s many people were opposed to the Scotsman's radical ideas. They argued that such safety devices would take away the romance from the sport. Stewart argued that these critics had never crashed at 150mph.

After BRM, Stewart moved back to Tyrrell, which was now competing in Formula One and, in 1969, he became World Champion; an achievement he matched in 1971 and 1973. He may also have won in 1972, but missed a number of races due to illness.

After 1973 Stewart retired from Formula One, following the death of his team-mate, Francois Cevert at Watkins Glen. He then went on to be a consultant for Ford before setting up his own Formula One team in 1997, alongside his son, Paul.

LEFT
Stewart taking the chequered flag at the 1973 Monaco Grand Prix.

FAR LEFT
Stewart in 1973, before the Monaco Grand Prix, wearing his trademark tartan helmet.

BELOW
Stewart at the 2004 Australian Grand Prix, watching his Jaguar team in action.

ewart Grand Prix was run in conjunction with Ford nd drivers included Rubens Barrichello and Johnny erbert. Sadly, the team didn't achieve any notable iccess before being taken over fully by Ford in 2000 nd renamed Jaguar Racing.

Most recently, Stewart has made a name for imself as a motorsport commentator on US levision, where viewers enjoy his distinctive ottish accent.

However, perhaps his greatest contribution to ormula One has been his relentless campaign to nprove safety. And for that, everyone involved in e sport should be grateful.

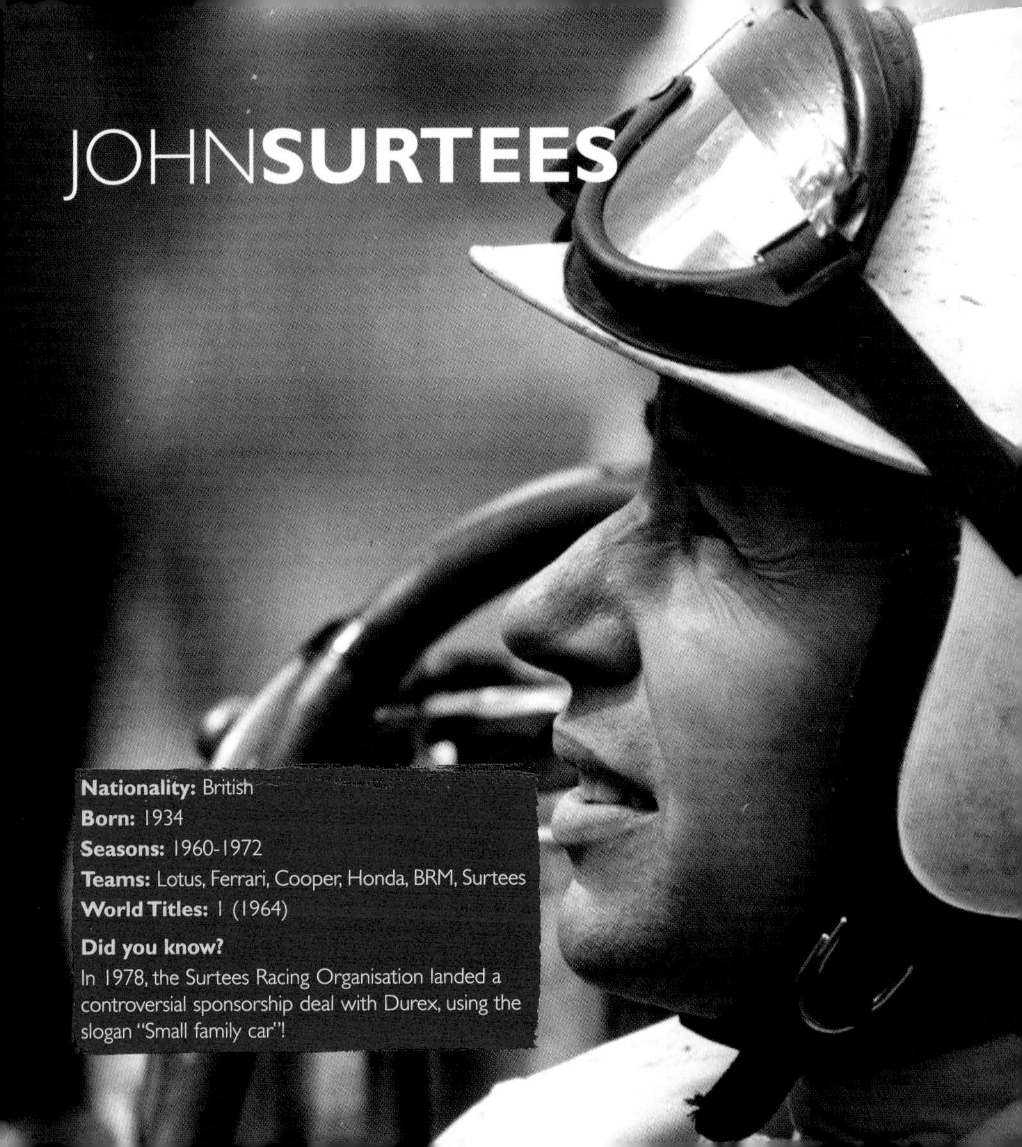

JOHN**SURTEES**

Nationality: British
Born: 1934
Seasons: 1960-1972
Teams: Lotus, Ferrari, Cooper, Honda, BRM, Surtees
World Titles: 1 (1964)

Did you know?

In 1978, the Surtees Racing Organisation landed a controversial sponsorship deal with Durex, using the slogan "Small family car"!

John Surtees has gone down in history as the only person ever to win the World Championship in both Formula One and Motorcycle Grands Prix. An impressive achievement. He started off on two wheels for the simple reason his father, Jack, owned a motorcycle shop in South London and was also three-time British motorcycle sidecar champion. The young Surtees got his first motorbike at the age of 11 and learnt, not only to ride it, but also to maintain the machine himself. He left school at the age of 16 and served as an apprentice engineer for Vincent, the British motorcycle manufacturer. Before long, Surtees competed in – and won – his first motorcycle race.

Surtees then went to race for Norton in 1955 and won an incredible 68 out of 76 races that year. He moved next to the Italian MV Agusta team and won seven World Championships between 1956 and 1960. This was undoubtedly a man who was hard to beat!

His achievements on two wheels gained the attention of car racing teams and the now-famous Surtees was great in demand. He didn't disappoint, either, when he was finally coaxed behind the wheel of a racing car. At his first single-seater event – at Goodwood in a Ken Tyrrell Formula Three Cooper – Surtees finished a close second to Jim Clark. Following this performance, Lotus's Colin Chapman signed him for the end of the 1960 season and Surtees came second at the British and Portuguese Grands Prix that year. Formula One teams were by then clamouring to sign him, so he made the decision to retire from motorcycle racing and concentrate on Formula One, racing first for Lotus.

However, it wasn't until Surtees moved to Ferrari, in 1963, that he really started to shine. As the team's number-one driver, he had his first victory at the Nürburgring; a win he repeated the following year. Indeed, 1964 was to be his finest season, with Surtees winning the battle for the

BELOW

Surtees in action at Silverstone in 1966, driving a Ferrari.

Championship against Graham Hill and Jim Clark. Victory at Mexico, at the end of the season, clinched the title for Surtees.

It was a great result but was also to be Surtees' last Championship title. In 1965, he moved to the USA to compete in the Can-Am series, driving his own Lola, while remaining with Ferrari. A bad crash in Canada led to him being badly injured, but he was soon back racing at the Belgian Grand Prix, where he drove superbly in heavy rain to one of his finest wins. That, though, was his last drive for Ferrari; for some time, he'd not got on with the team manager, Eugenio Dragoni, and stormed out on him one day, never to return. Apparently, Surtees later admitted to Enzo Ferrari that this had been a mistake for him and the team. Unfortunately, Surtees had developed a reputation for being argumentative and cantankerous, and did not suffer fools gladly.

Surtees joined the Cooper team in 1966 and drove their Maserati-engined car to victory in Mexico that year. Beyond that, though, he struggled with uncompetitive cars and, in 1969, moved to BRM. Again, though, the cars were not as reliable as he'd hoped and Surtees had little luck; a fact that was not helped by his own health problems, which dated back to that accident in Canada.

Fed up with other people's mechanical inadequacies, Surtees started his own Formula One team in 1970. The Surtees Racing

Organisation used V8 Cosworth engines and showed promise in the early years, with Surtees himself driving for the first two seasons. Other drivers included John Watson, Derek Bell and Alan Jones.

Long-term, the team struggled to survive, however, and ended up taking on pay drivers - people who paid for a chance to race in Formula One. Sadly, though, this was not enough to ensure survival and Surtees Racing withdrew from Formula One in 1978. The following year it competed briefly in Formula 5000 before going out of business for good.

John Surtees retired gracefully from motorsport at that time, and enjoyed life at a gentler pace in his Kent country house, his temper mellowed with age. A keen interest in architecture enabled him to be a successful property developer.

ABOVE
The Ferrari of John Surtees taking a corner at speed at Monte Carlo in 1965.

FAR LEFT
John Surtees in his Ferrari at the Syracuse Grand Prix of 1966.

GILLES**VILLENEUVE**

Nationality: Canadian
Born: 1950
Died: 1982
Seasons: 1977-1982
Teams: McLaren, Ferrari

Did you know?

Gilles Villeneuve's younger brother, Jacques, was also a successful racing driver. He drove briefly for the Arrows Formula One team in 1981, but had more success in snowmobile and CART racing. He is often called Uncle Jacques to differential him from his nephew, the Formula One driver of the same name.

Canadian driver Gilles Villeneuve may never have won the World Championship, but f it hadn't been for his untimely death, there's a good chance he would have done one day. As it is, he's remembered fondly for being a talented driver and has gone lone in history as a true legend.

From a very early age, the young Villeneuve was fascinated by anything mechanical nd loved to play with toy bulldozers and trucks; so long as they looked realistic. His persistent character showed early, too, as he struggled to learn to ride a bike without tabilisers. Not a natural pupil, the youngster preferred the outdoor life to school; he ode his bike in the summer and skated and played hockey through the winter.

At the age of nine, Villeneuve's father let him drive the family's Volkswagen van along a quiet road and, from that day on, the boy was hooked on cars, and by the time he was 15 ie was fixing up an old MGA, in readiness for being old enough to drive legally. In the neantime, though, he sneaked off in his father's Pontiac one night and illegally drove it to he nearby city. Travelling at speeds of over 100mph, Villeneuve lost control on the wet oads and crashed into a telegraph pole. The car was a write-off but, luckily, the teenager vas unhurt, and walked home in the rain to confess to his parents what had happened.

By the time he was 16, Villeneuve was once again behind the wheel – this time legally. Iowever, one day he was on his way to see his girlfriend when another car tarted to race him along the road. The eenager rose to the challenge and the race vas on. Until, that is, a herd of cows got n the way, and Villeneuve ended up in a litch, needing 80 stitches to his head.

The high-speed pursuit had excited 'illeneuve, despite his injuries, so he ought himself an old Skoda and was soon lying around the local roads, picking up nore than his fair share of speeding tickets.

Although fascinated by racing cars and lrivers, Villeneuve didn't have the money o pursue his dream, so he turned instead o snowmobile racing. His courage and

BELOW

Villeneuve takes team orders, 1982.

natural talent shone through and he was offered a job by a snowmobile manufacturer, demonstrating its products. He claimed afterwards that he learnt a lot about control, piloting snowmobiles at over 100mph on slippery surfaces.

Now in his early 20s and married with a baby son – Jacques – Villeneuve began racing in Formula Ford and was the Quebec Champion in 1973. Next, he tried his hand at Formula Atlantic, sinking all his money into it. In 1976, he dominated the Championship, despite not being able to afford to compete in every race, and took the title. This gave him plenty of much-needed publicity and he was offered a drive with McLaren for 1977.

He had a good first season and showed a lot of promise, but McLaren decided not to keep him on for another year. Instead, Ferrari stepped in and signed Villeneuve for 1978. He won his first race the following year; fittingly at the Canadian Grand Prix. In all, Villeneuve won Formula One races during his career and, in 1979, he finished second in the Championship.

By 1982, Villeneuve was widely regarded as the best driver in Formula One and tipped to be the Champion that year. However, the season got off to a bad start at San

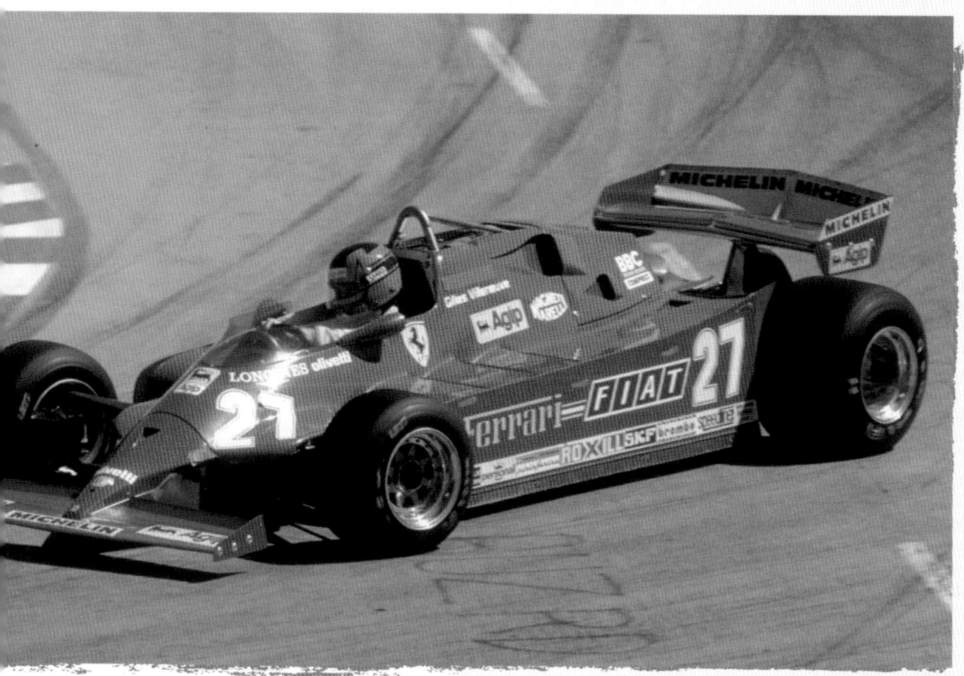

Marino when his teammate, Didier Pironi, disobeyed team orders and passed the Canadian, who was leading, thus depriving Villeneuve of a win.

At the next race of the season, at the Belgian Grand Prix at Zolder, disaster struck. During qualifying, Villeneuve's front left wheel touched the right rear wheel of another car. Villeneuve's Ferrari flew into the air and crashed, nose first, into an embankment, before cartwheeling along the side of the track. He died in hospital shortly afterwards.

Villeneuve may have been killed before he realised his full potential, but his memory lives on, and he still has a huge following around the world. His son, Jacques, took up where his father left off and won the World Championship in 1997.

ABOVE
Villeneuve takes one of the corners at the Monte Carlo Grand Prix, 1981.

FAR LEFT
Gilles Villeneuve sips champagne in the Race of Champions at Brands Hatch in the late 1970s.

JACQUES VILLENEUVE

Nationality: Canadian

Born: 1971

Seasons: 1996-

Teams: Williams, BAR, Renault, BMW Sauber

World Titles: 1 (1997)

Did you know?

In 1996, Jacques Villeneuve practiced for the Belgian Grand Prix at Spa by playing a computer game. However, in the game he could only manage to qualify in 18th place. When it came to the race itself, he achieved pole position!

acques Villeneuve will perhaps always be known as the son of Gilles Villeneuve, but ie has also been a successful driver in his own right, winning the World Championship in 1997. Jacques was only 11 years old when his father was killed in an horrific accident at the Belgian Grand Prix in 1982. His mother was not urprised when, at the age of 13, her son announced that he wanted to follow in his ather's footsteps and be a racing driver. She told him he could go karting if he did vell in his maths exam, a subject he was weak at. Relishing a challenge, the young Villeneuve worked hard at school, achieved good marks, and so his mother stuck to ier word.

The following year found Villeneuve at the Imola kart track in Italy, together with his ister Melanie. The boy started off driving a 100cc kart, and the instructors were so mpressed by his performance that they let him try a 135cc version. By the end of the lay, the teenager was driving a Formula Four car around the Grand Prix track. Racing was lefinitely in his blood!

His uncle, Jacques Villeneuve senior (often called Uncle Jacques) was also a racing lriver, and enrolled his nephew on a three-day course at the Jim Russell Driving School n Quebec. Once again, the instructors were impressed by the 15-year-old's ability behind he wheel. Indeed, one of them said that the boy was the best student they'd ver had.

Even so, the teenager was, at this stage, unsure whether he wanted to be a racing lriver, or pursue his other passion, which vas skiing. He decided to stick with cars, hough, and in 1989 Villeneuve began acing in the Italian Formula Three series. Despite some competent driving he didn't xcel, probably because of the cars he was lriving so, in 1992, he left to compete in he Japanese Formula Three Championship.

In Japan, he was free of the constant ublicity that surrounded the son of the

BELOW

Villeneuve locks his brakes in dramatic fashion during the Luxembourg Grand Prix in 1998.

famous Canadian and Villeneuve's driving improved immensely, with him finishing the season in second place. He then moved to the USA and took part in the Toyota Atlantic series, where he won five races. In 1994 he raced in Champ Car and was Rookie of the Year and, the following year, he won the Indianapolis 500 as well as the Championship title.

Villeneuve's success in the USA attracted the attention of Frank Williams who signed him for the 1996 season. It was a good move for the team because Villeneuve excelled himself by achieving pole position and a podium finish (second place) in his first Grand Prix, at Melbourne. In fact, he could have won the race, if team orders weren't to allow his teammate, Damon Hill, to pass. Villeneuve went on to win four races in his first season, gain 11 podium finishes and score 78 points – unprecedented results for a newcomer.

The next year was even better for Villeneuve. Now the number-one driver at Williams, he fought a season-long battle against Ferrari's Michael Schumacher, and claimed seven wins, eight podium finishes and 81 points. The battle for the Championship went right to the last race, in Australia, where Schumacher tried, unsuccessfully, to force Villeneuve out of the race. The plan backfired and the

LEFT

Villeneuve in a practice session for the Bahrain Grand Prix, 2006.

FAR LEFT

Jacques Villeneuve looks on, as his father Gilles is interviewed, 1974.

BELOW

Villeneuve talks to the media, 2005.

ierman ended up in the gravel and Villeneuve went n to win the race, clinching the title. An amazing chievement for someone so new to Formula One.

Sadly, Villeneuve has so far been unable to match is early years' achievements. After a disappointing eason with Williams in 1998, he moved to BAR in 999, where he struggled with technical problems. ven so, he stayed with the team until 2003, when e quit before the end of the season.

With no team to compete in for in 2004, illeneuve took time off, returning at the end of the eason to drive for Renault. At the same time, he gned a two-year deal with BMW Sauber, starting in 005. Whether Villeneuve ever does as well as he id in his first two seasons of Formula One remains be seen – he certainly deserves to.

ALSO AVAILABLE IN THIS SERIES

The Little Book of
CRICKET
LEGENDS
RALPH DELLOR and STEPHEN LAMB

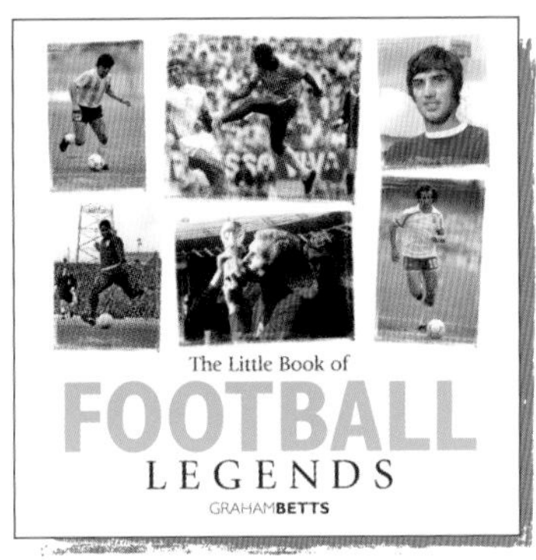

The Little Book of
FOOTBALL
LEGENDS
GRAHAM BETTS

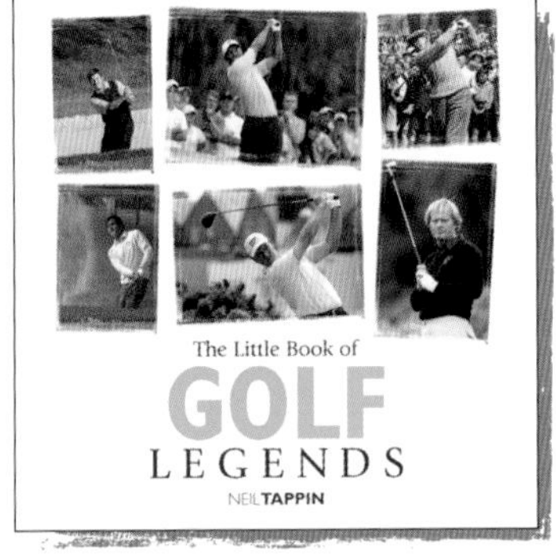

The Little Book of
GOLF
LEGENDS
NEIL TAPPIN

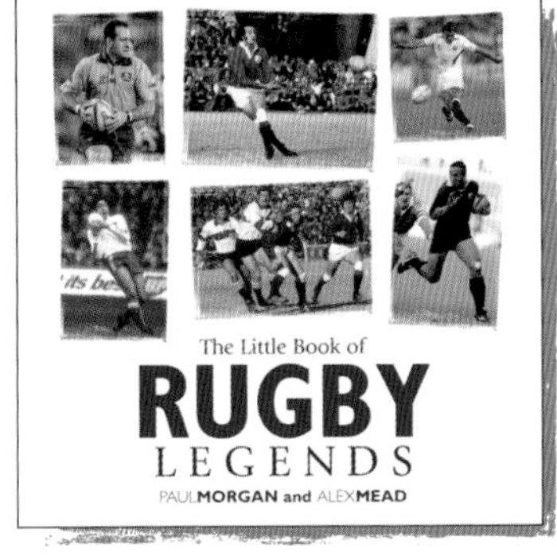

The Little Book of
RUGBY
LEGENDS
PAUL MORGAN and ALEX MEAD

THE PICTURES IN THIS BOOK WERE PROVIDED COURTESY OF THE FOLLOWING:

GETTY**IMAGES**
101 Bayham Street, London NW1 0AG

NATIONAL**MOTOR**MUSEUM
Beaulieu, Brockenhurst, Hampshire SO42 7ZN

Concept and Art Direction:
VANESSA **and** KEVIN**GARDNER**

Design and Artwork: KEVIN**GARDNER**

PUBLISHED BY GREEN UMBRELLA PUBLISHING

Publishers:
JULES**GAMMOND,** TIM**EXELL,** VANESSA**GARDNER**

Series Editor: VANESSA**GARDNER**

Written by: PHILIP**RABY**